THE SEVENTEEN
TRADITIONS

THE SEVENTEEN
TRADITIONS

LESSONS FROM AN
AMERICAN CHILDHOOD

RALPH NADER

ILLUSTRATIONS BY DAVID WOLF

HARPER

NEW YORK • LONDON • TORONTO • SYDNEY

HARPER

A hardcover edition of this book was published in 2007 by HarperCollins Publishers.

HarperCollins books may be purchased for educational, business, or sales promotional use. For information please write: Special Markets Department, HarperCollins Publishers Inc., 10 East 53rd Street, New York, NY 10022.

FIRST HARPER PAPERBACK PUBLISHED 2012.

Designed by Kris Tobiassen
Illustrations by David Wolf

Library of Congress Cataloging-in-Publication Data has been applied for.

ISBN 978-0-06-221064-7

12   13   14   15   16   RRD (H)   10   9   8   7   6   5   4   3   2   1

To my parents,
Nathra Nader and
Rose Bouziane Nader

To Shafeek, Claire, and Laura

And to young parents

CONTENTS

The Landscape of My Boyhood

The bell rang at Central School one early autumn day, signaling that our eighth-grade classes were over. The other schoolboys and I headed boisterously for the exit doors. As we passed a girl in our class, one of the boys cocked his head toward her, looked at us, and said pointedly, *"What a pig."*

She heard him, of course, and as I looked back I saw her shattered expression before she walked away. The boys just laughed loudly. "Ugh," one of them added, seconding the remark. I was stunned. This girl was one of our friendliest, and most helpful, classmates. We'd all been in the same class with her since the first grade. Everyone liked her. As I walked home, I found myself unable to shake off this sudden episode. What was her crime, I asked myself? She wasn't one of the beauties in our class, but was that her fault? Did she deserve this boy's casual cruelty? Nothing of this kind had happened when we were in the first, second, third, fourth, fifth, sixth, or seventh grades. Why now?

For the rest of that day and into the evening, I couldn't stop thinking about that girl's crestfallen expression, and the sneering, insensitive look on the boy's face. The fellow who'd made the comment wasn't a class bully or a loudmouth. But that afternoon, glancing at an innocent thirteen-year-old girl, he was hurtful to her. She was just another girl in the class, perhaps a little plain-faced and pale. What had she done to warrant his verbal fury? Was his real goal to impress us, by demonstrating that he knew who was attractive and who wasn't? Whatever the explanation, I suspected that the onset of puberty had taken over the boy's mind—that the lower half of his growing body was taking over his top half, where his brain lived, displacing years of looking at the girl for who she was and not how she looked. In this respect, that boy had been a better person at nine or ten than he was that day.

I'd like to think that my siblings and I weren't guilty of such behavior. But when we did act up, my mother had a standard response. Whenever she felt we'd let our baser instincts stop us from thinking for ourselves, she'd say, "I believe it's you." *There's nothing wrong with that girl,* she'd have told that thoughtless boy. *But there is something wrong with* you, *for prejudging her that way.* That always set us straight.

As an adult, I've often noticed how common it is for people to accept conventional, commercially driven definitions of human beauty—indeed, to accept conventional ideas of all kinds. And I've always been grateful to my childhood, in all its fullness, for teaching me to challenge preconceptions and reject conformity or coercion, those influences that inflict so much pain, deprivation, and tragedy upon our communities and societies today. Despite all my years of higher education at Princeton University and Harvard Law School, I might never have learned to think this way without the guidance of my parents, my family, and the small-town community where I grew up.

In these times of widespread conformity and self-censorship, I find myself thinking back upon my childhood, recalling what made it special for me and for my brother and sisters. Recently I've found myself thinking that I should share these memories with others, in the hope that they might offer guidance and inspiration for the parents, children, and grand-children of today. And what I hope will be especially helpful, in this very different world we inhabit, are my memories of the traditions in which my childhood was immersed—traditions that remain vivid in my mind, and that guide me to this day.

I am often asked what forces shaped me. Rather than trying to give a full answer to that question—which would take longer than a limited interview would allow—I often reply simply, "I had a lucky choice of parents." My brother, two sisters, and I had a remarkable father and mother, who cared for us in both direct and subtle ways. The examples of their lives set us on the solid paths we have explored ever since.

Among other things, my parents were responsible for passing down the traditions they had learned from the generations before them—traditions they refined and adapted to the unfamiliar country and culture to which they had emigrated early in the twentieth century. These traditions arose from the received wisdom and customs they had learned during their own childhoods in Lebanon, elaborated by their own judgments, sensibilities, and changing circumstances. In turn, they were nourished by regular feedback from their acculturating children, which they encouraged.

Mother and Father each lived to be just short of a century old; we benefited from their seasoned perspectives and wisdom for many, many years. They were forever young, exemplifying my mother's strong belief in the importance of remaining "interested and interesting." And they succeeded in doing this throughout their lives, attracting ever-younger friends to visit, whether we children were home or not. They created the strong family base from which my siblings and I sallied forth into the wider world, full of new experiences and high expectations.

That base was, in part, a matter of locale. My parents made a conscious choice to move to Winsted, a small town nestled in the Litchfield Hills of northwestern Connecticut, where I was born in the middle of the Depression.

Winsted was, and wasn't, a typical New England town. Through it ran the Mad River and the Still River, named by the settlers who arrived in those dense woods in the latter part of the eighteenth century. Connecticut is dotted with such mill towns, which depended on the rivers to power their factories. Most of these towns were small, dominated by one or two large factories. Winsted, on the other hand, had spawned a hundred factories and fabrication shops by 1900, and these factories in turn gave rise to homes, shops, and other businesses—including probably more drinking bars per square yard than any town east of the Mississippi. The town of Winchester, which includes Winsted, is shaped like a lopsided rectangle that angles from the southwest to the northeast. The land is very hilly with ridges, upland lakes, and the valley where most of the factories, stores, schools, and homes were located. When my father opened his restaurant-bakery along the town's mile-long Main Street, the local population was ten thousand, in an area roughly the size of Manhattan.

It was a walking town. In those days, youngsters didn't have to rely on Mama or Papa to drive them around. Nor were there school buses, except for the really distant rural homes. You walked. I walked. It was a good town for walking, with its tree-shaded streets, well-kept sidewalks, and access to just about everything for our needs, wants, and whims. Just a brisk walk away—no more than fifteen to twenty minutes—were the schools, the playgrounds, most of the homes, the town hall, the movie theater, the shops, the factories, the daily newspaper offices, the library, the historical society, the hospital and churches, police and fire departments, dentists, doctors, lawyers, the railroad station, the post office, the electric and telephone companies, and the county courtroom.

Winstedites could walk up nearby hills to visit the dairy farms where their milk came from, to relax at Highland Lake (the second largest natural lake in Connecticut), or to explore any number of quieter meadows, woods, and streams. It was a good community for families raising children, with no cement, asphalt, or skyscrapers sealing the people off from the land, the water, their beloved gardens, or the sky, with its breezes and horizons. Nature, unsequestered, inspired my mother to sing so often, "Oh, what a beautiful morning!"

My mother and father had both grown up in small communities themselves. My paternal grandfather died when my father was an infant. Dad grew up with his mother, sister, and brother in the little village of Arsoon, in the mountains of Lebanon. The swimming hole in Arsoon provided an inviting setting, and my father impressed the neighborhood boys with his diving skills every year. As children, we never tired of his stories about daring jumps into the cold mountain waters. Mother grew up in Zahle, a foothill town above Lebanon's fertile Bekaa Valley, the country's breadbasket. She was the fourth daughter in a family of eight girls. My grandparents took four cousins under their wing and raised them along with their own children.

Our parents' families preserved both their own traditions, passed down by their ancestors, and newer traditions learned from their experiences with foreign occupation—first the Ottoman Turks, then the French. Our parents always stressed that the best from the old should be merged with the best from the new. Winsted's other immigrant families—Irish, Italian, Polish, and other Eastern Europeans, who worked in the textile, hardware, and clock factories and shops—seemed to feel the same way. Grown-ups and children spent far more time with each other than is the case today, and the wisdom flowed freely between them.

Winsted was a true community, known for its frequent parades and lively public life. The sidewalks of Main Street were often bustling with townspeople shopping and doing their errands. Neighbors knew each other well and visited regularly, for television had not yet arrived. Most of the national service clubs and associations of those years, such as the Veterans of Foreign Wars, the Rotary, the Kiwanis, the Lions, the Elks, the Knights of Columbus, the Red Cross, the Masons, the Salvation Army, the YMCA, had chapters in town. Most factory workers were able to afford a mortgage on a modest house and a second-hand car, if not a new one, and after World War II federal housing assistance programs helped the returning veterans make their way. Situated snugly in the picturesque Litchfield Hills, Winsted—then the seat of Litchfield County—enjoyed the status of being the last stop on the railroad line from New York City. Until the 1940s, seven trains left Winsted for the Big City each day. It was like being at the headwaters of a mighty river— one that flowed both ways.

Winsted also had the reputation of a town where argument flourished. It was known for its noisy town meetings, and for the heady conversations that erupted constantly in its bars, restaurants, and grocery stores, not to mention the post office and the town hall. The town still followed the New England town meeting tradition, in which residents voted each year to approve—or disapprove—the budget. The people of Winsted weren't inclined to delegate their rights to elected representatives. Instead they aired their concerns in a constant stream of public debate, much of which found its way into the local newspaper, the *Winsted Evening Citizen*. Our town was one of the smallest in the country with its own daily newspaper, and the residents took full advantage of the megaphone it afforded them.

Winsted had the misfortune of enduring a recurrent natural disaster, courtesy of the Mad River, whose waterpower encouraged the construction of several factories on its banks. Again and again, though, the Mad River overflowed those banks, giving rise to three generations of catastrophic floods that culminated in a devastating hurricane-fed wall of water that socked the town in August 1955. Each new flood led to innumerable problems, and innumerable questions for the townspeople to grapple with—a veritable reservoir of municipal conflict, resolution, or procrastination.

Yet Winsted never seemed cowed by the regular assaults of the Mad River. For a town of its size, it produced an impressive array of long-lasting philanthropic institutions, including the Litchfield County Hospital, the Beardsley and Memorial Library, the Gilbert School, and the grassroots charity known as the Volunteer Winsted Fire Department.

The town's givers were matched, of course, by its takers—led by the industrial factories, which were low-paying and vigorously anti-union. The older companies were always vigilant about keeping new union factories out of the area. They seemed equally determined to keep fresh air and water at bay, using those two resources as their pollution sinks and sewers. The original factories were not very charitable institutions. And in the 1950s many of their founders' descendants lost their competitive spirit and sold out to absentee owners, who soon moved or closed down their acquisitions. By the time my siblings and I were off at college, Winsted was evolving from a diverse, self-contained mill town to a bedroom town, full of workers who commuted to jobs in Hartford, Torrington, and Waterbury. The air and water became cleaner after the factories closed, but the toxic soils and hollowed-out buildings remained, economic tripwires to any prospects of new development in the area.

As with many such communities, Winsted in those years was marked by ethnic and religious divisions, and these in turn were linked to economic hierarchies. In those years, the town was 99 percent white. There was a calm, though by no means complete, social self-segregation between the Protestant and Catholic families, preserved by the memberships of the town's large Catholic church and the four Protestant churches. There was little bitter overt hostility between the groups; for better or worse, people knew their social place. Civically, on the other hand, all bets were off. The first generation of immigrants knew that the old-line Yankees ran the town and controlled the economy, but with each decade their children and grandchildren asserted more and more political power, and by the 1950s the Yankee industrialists' children were leaving town for more affluent communities.

My boyhood in this small town was shaped by my family, my friends, our neighbors, my chores and hobbies, the town's culture and environment, its schools, libraries, factories, and businesses, their workers, and by those storms that came from nowhere to disrupt everything. All these things defined my mental landscape. Yet childhood in any family is a mysterious experience, one that transcends its most obvious parts. What are the elements that influence human development? Water, air, and nutrition interact with genetic material to develop the body, including the brain. But what shapes the mind, the personality, the character? Try explaining why one sister or brother comes out so differently from the others when they all were raised in the same household, by the same parents, under the same economic, social, educational, and recreational circumstances. Mysterious it is, but that only makes the process more fascinating.

Years later, I came to realize that my own experience as a child had been touched very deeply by certain objects that were part of my natural surroundings—objects that stimulated my senses and mind in a lasting way. As a little boy I embraced their presence, and allowed them to usher me into an intimate world of imagination, curiosity, reverie, wonder, and awe. They afforded me a sense of solitude, quietude, and comfort; they served as speechless hosts for my childhood communion.

During my early teens, my older brother, Shafeek, gave me a book by James Harvey Robinson, the noted social and intellectual historian. Much of the book was beyond my years, but one thing in this slim volume remained with me—Robinson's emphasis on the importance of reverie in daily life. As I entered adulthood, I found that reverie became harder and harder to achieve in any given day, in our society of instant communication, fast food, fast commuting, and ever faster ways for everything.

By the early 1970s, we were well on our way to the total immersion experience of the television age, in which most children watched thirty to forty hours of TV a week. They read less and their vocabulary decreased. The decades that followed saw the arrival of twenty-four-hour cable television, VCRs, home computer games, and the Internet—each in turn cementing the place of the TV screen in our children's lives. In those years I remember reading about the Fresh Air Fund, a program that offers New York City's poor children a chance to spend a few summer weeks in the countryside. For many of these children it was the first time that they had ever walked on soil, on earth! It was the first time they smelled fresh cut grass and hay. For some, it was the first time they'd seen an authentic sunset, not just the televised variety. Today, children everywhere are deprived of exposure to nature in the same way; they grow up with their eyes, ears, tastes, and other senses trained on a corporate world of sensual virtual reality—removed, as no other generation in human history, from the daily flow and rhythm of nature.

How very different were my early years, lived so close to nature's bounty. When I reflect back on the importance of my family and my childhood, I find that my mind often floods with imagery from these natural surroundings that stirred my imagination in those years. What became a little world to me, as an adult, was a very large world to me as a child. Nature has its own power, drawing us into its magical ambience. And I remember it vividly:

FIRST, THERE WERE SOUNDS . . .

A child does not take sounds for granted. Especially nature's sounds, emanating from unseen or mysterious sources. Repetition never dulls their music.

An old-timer down at the school ballyard once told me that no creature in the animal or insect kingdoms makes a sound without a purpose. As a child, I challenged myself to separate one sound from the next, distinguishing them as birdwatchers do. On summer nights, it was nearly impossible to pick out the strands of the cacophony that drifted in from the fields, bushes, and trees—so many creatures were engaged in their ritualistic recitals. But I listened as the peepers and crickets talked with one another. I even tried to hear the lightning bugs, the fireflies, though they remained silent in their inscrutable luminosity.

Other sounds were harder to ignore. I never enjoyed the barking of the neighborhood dogs, the neurotic domesticated canines whose incessant yelping interrupted the feral sounds of the outdoors. But the most perceptibly urgent and haunting sounds were the high-pitched snarls of the cats at mating time. Before the birds and bees were explained to me, I knew what these tomcats were up to. They kept me awake more than a few nights. I much preferred the sounds of the primeval woods and fields, especially the long howling winds as they swirled through hills and valleys, swaying the trees and bending the tall grasses.

There were other songs that rang true to my ears. The daily mooing of cows on the hilly outskirts of town reminded us that soon the dairy farmers would deliver their fresh milk. The splashing and gurgling of nearby brooks and streams seemed as though it had been ongoing for thousands of years. As I sat by these flowing waters, waiting to see a fish here and a tadpole or frog there, my schoolboy's patience paled in comparison with those eternal waves.

THEN THERE WAS THE MAPLE TREE . . .

Directly in front of the stairs leading to our house stood a magnificent maple, more than sixty-five feet tall. Its branches spread before my bedroom window, and they were my four distinct seasons, my wildlife menagerie, and my mystery forest, all in one. In the springtime its leaves sprouted and matured quickly, inviting squirrels to climb and leap around with abandon. Its interior spaces hosted birds of every variety—imperious crows, friendly chickadees, stately blue jays, motherly robins, hardheaded woodpeckers, frequent sparrows, even the occasional cardinal. I watched them flitting about on the smaller branches and twigs, and wondered about the meaning of their calls to one another. The effusive crows would wake me up with their

insistent territorial sparring. When it got too loud, I would slam the window shut.

With the coming of the New England autumn, the leaves turned dazzling colors, and when they fell, they turned the road, lawns, and sidewalks into a carpet of leafy beauty. I loved walking through their ankle-deep drifts, kicking the fragrant, starchy leaves into the air or collecting the best ones to place in my schoolbooks. Our street was full of large maple trees, so the fall produced a canopy of brilliant hues high above the street where the trees meshed with one another across both sides of the road to form their protective ceiling. Even today, just the crunch or rustle of fallen leaves underfoot kindles within me a nostalgia for those days of bonding with the ebb and flow of the seasons.

Yet nothing could quite match the beauty of this maple a

few weeks later, when wet snowflakes clung to its bark in the early morning hours after the season's first snowfall. The maple in wintertime became a sound tunnel for the symphony of wind, as it fluttered and whistled, then growled and howled. It synchronized nature's forces into a veritable orchestra for my young ears. The maple was so strong and deeply rooted that no winter wind or hurricane gust ever stripped anything more than an exposed twig from its mooring. We never named the tree, but for me it had a personality nonetheless; I associated it with a cluster of mysteries I imagined while lying in bed next to my outdoor companion. In my eleventh year we grew closer, once I was tall and strong enough to latch on to the lowest sturdy branch and swing back and forth. The following year, still taller, I learned how to climb this giant, scrambling ever higher into its skyward reaches—while my mother stood below, reminding me to respect the law of gravity.

THEN THERE WERE THE FRUIT TREES . . .

The maple was only the largest of the many trees in my childhood landscape. The green apple tree in our yard was easy to climb, easier to sit on, but the apples bordered on mangled. Worms got them, bugs got to them. Only a few apples at a time were good enough to eat, but the scarcity had its own appeal: To find an apple that was edible was a treat, all the more enjoyable because it was a surprise.

The pear tree, just a few feet from our kitchen, was something else. This wasn't a tree for climbing. It had more serious business, which was to produce a regular crop of delicious pears every year. To this day I can taste the juices of the pears I plucked from its reachable branches or picked up from the ground. During the winter, my mother let us savor the preserves from the tree's overflowing harvest. It was such a sweetie of a tree, demanding nothing but some sun and rain and producing in return its wondrous fruit for some forty years before it gave out. As a young Yankee fan, I couldn't help likening it to the "old faithful" of my team, the clutch-hitting first baseman Tommy Henrich.

We even had a Concord grape arbor. Its output was erratic, but when it ripened, the large purple grapes were both very juicy and very sour—far better to look at than to devour.

THEN THERE WAS THE GARDEN . . .

Near the large field behind our street was our garden, where my parents planted an assortment of vegetables in our very rocky New England soil. The pebbles and stones were countless; I knew this firsthand, because one of my chores was to clear them out to make room for the tomatoes, lettuce, cucumbers, string beans, rhubarbs, radishes, parsley, and squash. I learned to admire farmers whose families had to care for so many acres of planted furrows and orchards when I realized how much work it took to manage our plot, which was the size of a large living room.

One summer, when I was nine or ten, a mysterious unseen creature took a keen liking to the lettuce plants in our garden. I was appointed the lookout for whatever omnivorous beast was raiding our crop. Soon enough I spotted a rabbit happily chewing away in our little plot, and I gave chase. The rabbit took off, but I gamboled off after him, holding a large rock in my hand. When I finally overtook him, the trespassing herbivore suddenly froze and looked frightfully at his towering assailant. I lofted the stone in the air, aiming at him from less than four feet away. For a few seconds I just stood there, breathing hard from the run, my hand suspended overhead. I saw those wide open eyes, and the crouching bunny to whom they belonged. But something held me back.

Finally, I put down the rock and turned back. The rabbit scampered, then hopped away. I could not explain what had happened in my mind, except that it had a lot to do with the image of a dead rabbit, its eyes closed. Looking back on that moment today, I know that that's when I realized I would never be a hunter—perhaps seeding my interests in safety, health, and conservation. I learned something about myself on that day of no regrets—among other things, that there were ways to defend a lettuce patch without destroying an innocent rabbit nibbling its meal.

THEN THERE WAS THE ROCK . . .

Not every friend I made in childhood could be found in my yard. One unlikely companion was just a few minutes' walk away—a boulder I came to think of as "the rock."

I discovered the rock as a boy of four, and immediately felt a kinship with it. Sometime in the late nineteenth century, it had been placed within the spacious grounds of the Soldier's Monument in the town of Winchester, where Winsted was located. Built to memorialize three hundred soldiers, including several dozen who died in the Civil War, the monument was an imposing, three-story, sixty-three-foot Gothic Revival structure on a two-acre hilltop spread donated by a local benefactor.

The rock sat near the circular dirt road that rounded the monument. More times than I can remember, my mother would give me a sandwich or an apple, and off I would scamper to eat it on my rock. It was some four feet high and about as wide; to a boy of four it seemed larger. But clambering up to the side of the rock was easy, and at the top was a comfortable seat. All kinds of insects seemed to love to crawl over the rock, and I took great joy in following their trails, noting their amazing variety and knack for

coexistence. On a clear evening I could look up at the stars from that perch, wondering what was out there. When it was cool on a sunshiny day, I would hug the rock for warmth.

As a ten-year-old, I flew kites from the rock, unleashing hundreds of feet of string as my brightly colored kites soared in the brisk breeze high above the woods and houses in the eastern part of town. Sometimes I couldn't control the pull on the kite, and the string would leap from my grasp or break clean off. When I finally got it stabilized as high as it would go, though, I would tie the string to an iron tether ring—driven into the rock during the horse-and-buggy days—and watch it fly.

I never attributed any mystical or animistic qualities to the old rock. In its mute solidity it was simply a place to be, a place to rest, a place to play, a place to dream.

THEN THERE WERE THE WOODS . . .

In colonial times, the woods of northwestern Connecticut were considered nearly impenetrable. In my youth they were still plenty dense, but negotiable in our daily walk to school. Half the fun was getting there, whether I went alone or with a school chum or two. Once we were out the back door, we headed up a flight of steps, through a field, across a pair of small roads, past the monument, and then we plunged into the woods. Downhill we went, over old stone walls, past a small but intriguing cave, through a thicket of trees and bushes, until we reached the resi-

dential street that led to the Central School. Wet, dry, snow drifts, butterflies, birds, rodents, birch trees, high grasses, ledges, trails, shafts of sunshine, gusts of wind—it all took a few minutes, but the woods were never tiresome and always engrossing. There was always a piece of wood to whittle, a dead branch to strip and to turn into a staff, a smooth stone to hurl high through the trees, mica to astonish, a snake to slither away at the sound of our footsteps, or a granite foothold to leap from as we hurtled down the wooded slope. It was fun, liberating, and when the snows turned into drifts just a little perilous, our school day was made a little more adventuresome.

THEN THERE WERE THE FIELDS . . .

The fields and the meadows were for romping, just romping, jumping, skipping, and rolling in the grass. They were for inspecting beetles and chasing grasshoppers, marveling at butter-flies and plant-circling bumblebees and other pollinators, and staring at the incredible hovering hummingbirds. Meadows were for pulling out blades of stiff grass and humming tunes with them. They were for spotting ants and anthills and crawling closer to watch their amazing, selfless work instincts and drive to bring food or their fallen kin back to their underground lairs. Ants never seemed to get discouraged, no matter how many times they were thwarted—a trait that did not escape my notice, even at the age of seven.

Ralph Waldo Emerson once defined a weed as a plant whose virtues were yet to be discovered, and in those days before herbicides and lawncare firms, we never gave a thought to the difference between grasses and weeds. Dandelions were beautiful to me, as were a large variety of flowers—daisies, black-eyed Susans, day lilies, jack-in-the-pulpits, whether they were in vogue or not. I made a study of their petals and stems, and of the busy, focused insects that were attracted to them.

THEN THERE WERE THE LAKES . . .

Near our home were two lakes—the recreational Highland Lake, and Crystal Lake, a smaller lake, on even higher ground, that served as our precious drinking water reservoir. Crystal Lake was just to be seen—no fishing or swimming. The town officials wanted to keep it as pure as possible. Highland Lake was another matter, and it was crowded with boats and swim-

mers, cottages and year-round homes. Polio was the great fear for many mothers of that period; doctors weren't yet completely sure of how the disease was spread, and many gave stern instructions to keep children away from crowded beaches. So I didn't swim very often in our lake, but we did motor or, with my two sisters and brother, walk around some of its seven miles of circumference. What excited me most as a little fellow were the spillways. The lake would spill over the road at two points, cascading down to the fast-moving Mad River a quarter mile below. My father would drive through the spillway waters, and to me, those five seconds of spraying water made it feel like we were on a brief ocean voyage.

Things sure look big when you're small.

THEN THERE WERE THE RIVERS . . .

The two rivers that crisscrossed our town's valley, the Still River and the Mad River, were troubled waters of different kinds. The appropriately named Mad River was the longtime source of several Main Street–destroying floods. But for decades it had also been receiving the bulk of the sewage from the towns and factories on its banks. The Still River, in like fashion, seethed with such an assortment of chemical dyes from the bordering textile and other factories that it looked at times like a botched rainbow.

As a result, there was no fishing to be had in these rivers, no swimming or picnics by their banks. The industries there and upstream had long since taken control, using these rivers as their sewers and dumping grounds, stealing the watery arteries from generations of Winstedites. Back then, most townspeople assumed that rivers were primarily for receiving waste—so much so that few of us seemed to feel robbed of our rivers. Without them, we were told, the plants would have never been built there. Worse yet, the standing pollution from the factories gave the town government little incentive to process its own municipal sewage. The rise of the environmental movement, and the cries of "Hey, these are *our* rivers," were still years away.

We still had many lessons to learn.

THEN THERE WAS THE SNOW . . .

When I say snow, I mean huge snowfalls—twenty to thirty inches at a time, sometimes piled on top of earlier drifts. I can still feel the swirls of wind-drenched snow filling my ears, neck, nose (I never liked hats, gloves, or scarves), the huge drifts we would plunge into with squealing bravado, and the endless shoveling of walks, stairs, and driveways. Sleds we used in order to go down moderate or steeper hills. But nothing could match up with what we called the "huge jump." The portal to the Soldier's Monument was a structure that was made of stone and looked like a giant quadrangular chess rook. It was probably about fifteen feet high. When the snow drifts reached six or seven feet, we would climb up to the top and jump into the drifts, our little bodies nearly disappearing into the deep pits our momentum created. Then we would go back and do it again. Snow, for us, was never something to be avoided. It was to be relished, battled, tackled, and deployed for sliding, plunging, and molding into different forms and shapes.

Our New England schools almost never closed. Except for the few who came from miles away, most of the students walked to school. Whatever the weather, we were expected to tough it out. Today, two- or three-inch dustings commonly close some urban and suburban schools. But when I was a boy, a good snowfall still brought out the best in us—among the children, who weren't afraid to trudge through a snowbank to get to school, and among the adults, who felt more obliged as neighbors to shovel their sidewalks—sidewalks that were used back then far more than now. It was a matter of pride.

THEN THERE WERE THE STARS . . .

Today the sight of stars has been abolished from city skies, debauched as they are by pollution, neon, and streetlights. From

Winsted's hills, during the early 1940s, we could see the stars with a clarity that allowed us to identify many of them without difficulty. The North Star, the Big Dipper, and the Little Dipper were familiar sights in our sky throughout the year.

For me, the stars were replete with fantasy, wish, wonder, with a sense of awe at the vastness, even eeriness, of the unknown. They stirred sentiments that exhilarated me as surely as many people are moved by great music. As I reclined on the rock, lay half-asleep outside on our porch, or just stood on our lawn, I found the stars nearly overwhelming. *Are those stars or planets?* I wondered. *How far away are they? Do people live on them? Do they really spin around or move at incredible speeds? Could they ever smash into the Earth?* Everything around me seemed to melt away at the sight of the stars. Though I was too little to put it into words, I was already feeling a sense of fascination with the idea of infinity, and with the ultimate secrets of the universe. And those ideas were real—not something that could be turned on and off with a remote control, no screen to keep me at a distance from nature's reality.

Did living this way—embedded not within a cacophony of electronic visualization and flashy advertisements, but within the natural world—make a difference?

It did for one little boy growing up in northwestern Connecticut.

*   *   *

Of course, I didn't have this landscape all to myself. In fact, as the baby of the family, I was sometimes the last in line to appreciate nature's wonders. But the embrace of my family, and my status as the youngest, gave me many advantages. I was following a path already traveled by my parents Rose and Nathra, my older brother, Shafeek, and my two sisters, Claire and Laura. As the last in line, I took a lot of ribbing. But somehow that only made me more observant and responsive to my elders.

My father had come to this country by steamship in 1912, at the age of nineteen. He had twenty dollars in his pocket, but he had confidence in his abilities, and a willingness to work hard. His first job was in Detroit, doing piecework at an automobile factory. From there he worked in one of the large textile mills in Lawrence, Massachusetts, a short time after the historic labor upheavals of those years. Then he moved to Newark, New Jersey, where he became a small distributor of groceries in that kinetic multiethnic melting pot. He had always intended to start his own business, and finally started a grocery store in Danbury, Connecticut. But he wanted to live in a smaller town, for he believed that a family would be best served by a place where people knew each other and life was more stable, less chaotic and disruptive.

In the early 1920s, my father returned to Lebanon. When he came back to Connecticut in 1925, with his nineteen-year-old bride, he found just the kind of place he wanted in the town of Winchester, which includes the town of Winsted. Winchester fit the measurements of the *polis,* the ideal small city-state outlined by the ancient Greeks. Pop found a building he liked on Main Street in Winsted, a building with upstairs apartments and a storefront on the ground level. He rented out the apartments, and below he opened up the Highland Sweet Shop, which eventually became a full-service restaurant and bakery he called the Highland Arms.

My mother was a standout student. After graduation she quickly became a teacher, first in her hometown and then in a nearby town—already an adventurous move for those times, when single women were to remain under their family's roof until they married. At that time village school boards tested a teacher's knowledge publicly before hiring, an event mother recalled with amusement over how she handled the challenge. Within months influenza struck that community and many of her students were stricken. Against all advice, mother insisted on visiting each of her students at home. She attributed some of her immunity to huge doses of raw garlic and fresh oranges daily. In her adopted country she gave birth to four children in her first nine years of marriage, and assumed the twin role of mother and active community-minded citizen.

Her first born, Shafeek (which means "the compassionate one" in Arabic), was wise beyond his years as a youngster. He took responsibility as a family duty. He loved exploring Winsted and the surrounding towns, farms, forests, and lakes with map in hand. He was the unusual big brother who took a continual interest in his younger siblings—in our well-being, our education, and our horizons. When he went off to the Navy in World War II, we felt like we were losing our coach—our source of curiosity and adventure, the older brother who taught us to dream about unusual futures.

Claire was the classic big sister. She filled in when my mother was preoccupied with other family or community matters, making sure I ate my food and did my chores. A selfless child, she regularly tended to the needs of others. During the war we raised chickens for their eggs and meat, and Claire disliked—indeed abhorred—plucking the feathers off a chicken we were preparing to have for dinner. But she found other joys in life, among them playing the piano.

Laura was an independent, mischievous child. When she was about two years old, she wriggled out of her carriage when no one was looking; my mother found her calmly trying to pet an unusually sociable black garden snake in the backyard. She was a runner, and very independent; she liked going where no one in the family had yet gone. But she also loved her sleep, and her piano lessons, and the banana split sundaes her big brother made for her in the restaurant.

Together we made a nicely balanced family, a mutually enriching group who enjoyed and benefited from each moment we spent together. Like nature itself, a family has certain built-in purposes: to protect its members, to nurture its children, to propagate itself so that it survives and thrives from generation to generation. Historically, the family is also the channel through which traditions are conveyed. In the distant past, traditions were shaped and enforced by larger groups—tribes, clans, and sects—from the top down, gradually trickling down through the extended family and then the nuclear family. Often this was done through social sanctions, sometimes with an iron fist. Today, except for some extended first-generation immigrant families, the job of passing down traditions is left to the nuclear family, and to many broken two-parent collaborations. Without the support of a strong community, the family is on its own, often forced to handle its regenerative and comforting functions while dealing with everything from economic insecurity and long work hours to the omnipresent commercialization of childhood.

Family, in short, is a gift. If you tried to put a value on all the functions American families perform, as though they were being purchased in the commercial marketplace, their total cost would compare favorably with the gross national product. Indeed, outsourcing family services to the market is already a formidable industry. And it will become more common unless we take to heart the intangible, noncommercial role that functional families play in the spiritual and material lives of our children. As helpful as many family services are, they can no more substitute for the real thing than the purchase of infant formula can replace the gift of natural mother's milk.

In our fast-moving contemporary society, the mounting external pressures felt by most families are eroding their ability to protect and nourish their children—to offer the guidance that helps children to face the world around them. Still, I believe this tide can be turned. The most devastated families in our history—those who survived the serial brutality of slavery—managed in many heroic instances to pass their traditions from one generation to the next, even as their oppressors tried every means they had to stop them. This resilience, under horrendous conditions, is a testament to the primordial, universal human need to invest the raising of our children with meaning, and with a sense of connectedness to the world around them.

As I look back on my own childhood, I realize how fortunate we were that our parents understood their own familial pasts, and that the traditions they observed in their own families would offer them an important framework as they tried to give their children healthy roots and prepare them for stable, well-directed lives in their new country. And so, in these pages, I have tried to capture some of my family's traditions as I experienced them in childhood and recall them today. I share them not as recipes or prescriptions, but as stimuli for your own thoughts and recollections—as an occasion to revisit lessons passed on within your own family. Such family traditions challenge the notion that the fads, technologies, how-to manuals, and addictions of modern life have somehow taken the place of the time-tested wisdom fashioned in the crucibles of earlier generations.

central Argument

The garb may change, after all, but the wearer does not.

1.

The Tradition
of Listening

One day, when she was in her mid-eighties, my mother and I were flying to California. Seated behind us was a young man. He started speaking with his seatmates before the doors to the airplane closed; kept talking as the plane took off; and was heard chatting over the Alleghenies, the Great Plains, the Rocky Mountains, the fertile California valleys, and into San Francisco. He never stopped talking, except to gulp down a meal and visit the restroom. When we landed, Mother turned to me.

"He didn't learn much in the past five hours, did he?" she said.

Listen more than you speak, and think before you speak my mother told us from the time we were old enough to do either, and over time we heard her until it was no longer necessary. To our parents, other children seemed to talk too much, and much of it was sheer nonsense and mischief that went well beyond the normal exuberance of youth. That wasn't going to happen with their offspring. My mother was determined to make sure all her children knew how to listen—not because she wanted to discipline us, or because she put a premium on peace and quiet, but because she wanted us to learn.

Learning how to listen was a core, if subtle, part of our early education. Mother gave us endless opportunities to listen, as she poured history, insight, advice, neighborhood events, and family stories from her ancestors into our absorbing minds. She also reenacted in installments celebrated sagas such as the story of Joan of Arc, and drew on her memories of dramatic historical events and their meaning for the present.

Both my mother and my father grew up in the folk culture of Lebanon, before the era of radio and television, before even electricity had arrived in their midst. There were no distant voices channeled into their living rooms or headphones. Instead their listening came from two sources: other human beings and nature itself, all of it obviously nearby. For example, one ever-present sound in their lives was the braying of donkeys, found trudging everywhere, carrying their masters and all kinds of loads. An entire folklore embracing donkey stories and jokes—often featuring a peasant foil named Jeha, along with the classic fables of Bidpai—was part of the storytelling inheritance they absorbed daily. If you didn't listen, how could you remember these jokes to share with your friends? It wasn't as if there were donkey joke websites to refresh their memories. The ear sharpens the memory, and my parents' generation had a trained capacity for listening during the interactions of daily life, if only because they had no alternatives.

Our father's emphasis on listening came from another direction—from his interest in politics and justice. He knew the importance of seeing things counterintuitively, of skeptical observation, and he taught us to follow his example by subjecting us to Socratic questioning in any given setting. Even his passing conversation made us want to listen; his remarks were so interesting. He was especially piquant on matters of money and charity. "Far more people know how to make big money than know how to spend it in useful ways," he once told us. "After they pile it up, they hardly know what to do with it, except spoil their descendants." Learning how to listen became a form of discipline that was rewarding in itself. It was not inhibiting; we still talked quite a bit. Our parents still listened quite a bit. But we four children never overwhelmed the conversation.

We learned to listen when guests were in the living room conversing with our parents. We learned to listen in school, which helped us avoid the restlessness of our schoolmates and enabled us to be more contemplative. We learned to listen to the evening radio network news, which sometimes had real relevance to our family—most memorably with the Pearl Harbor attacks of December 7, 1941, since my brother Shaf was nearing draft age. And we learned to listen to the spirited debates at the local town meetings and other public gatherings, instead of fidgeting and distracting our parents from their focus on the matters at hand.

My inclination for listening was a boon during the tens of thousands of miles I covered while hitchhiking. Half a century ago, hitchhiking was far more common—and safer—than it is today, and plenty of cars and trucks stopped to pick me up as I thumbed my way around the country. After a few introductory words, their drivers probably expected me to doze off for the balance of the trip. Instead, I saw every driver as an expert on some subject in his own right—whether he was a bricklayer, teacher, tree surgeon, factory worker, waiter, salesman, or a rug cleaner—and after asking an opening question or two, I just sat back, listened closely, and got a dose of enlightenment about each driver's life's skill or passion. My only regret is that I didn't carry a diary to write down some of the things I heard on these trips; still, what I did learn added up to a free extracurricular education—one that helped me interact with and understand a far broader selection of people than I would ordinarily have encountered as a high school, college, or law student.

Listening didn't always mean remaining silent. I learned early that good listening meant asking leading questions, and inserting verbal nudges that would tease out what you were really interested in learning. That early training helped me develop both my interviewing skills, which helped me throughout my career, and my patience in the long, often contentious, question-and-answer periods following my lectures and speeches. After sitting through one of these sessions, some reporters have written about what they call my "remarkable endurance." To me it has never been a matter of endurance, but rather the fruit of my family's tradition of listening in an effort to understand where other people were coming from.

As we grew older, we learned to listen and respond to the arguments of others who disagreed with us. Especially when we were young, Mother and Father made it clear that incessant talking obstructed the mind from receiving new information and improving itself. She encouraged us, in the fullest sense of the phrase, to keep an open mind. "The more you talk, the less you'll have to say," she would remind us. "The more you listen, the more sensible will be what you say."

2.

The Tradition of the Family Table

The *Wall Street Journal* once devoted an entire editorial to the subject of my mother. After another paper ran a story noting that she sometimes sent us off to school with a handful of chickpeas—instead of candy, presumably—and scraped the sugary frosting off of birthday cakes, the *Journal* took my mother to task for her "puritanical" ways. We did not take exception to my mother's attitudes toward food; in fact, the cake-scraping eventually became a family joke. For some bizarre reason, though, she evidently got under the skin of the hidebound reactionaries at the *Journal.* (Maybe they'd just run out of complaints against me.)

My mother was highly amused by the screed. She was so far ahead of them and their adherents regarding what food is all about. And what it's all about is not just food. For Mother, the family table was a mosaic of sights, scents, and tastes, of talking and teaching, of health, culture, beauty, history, stimulation, and delight. For Dad, it was a time to pepper us with questions, never thinking for a moment that they might have been over our heads. *So what about the leader theory of history?* he would ask. *Do leaders make changes, or do they largely reflect dynamic pressures on the ground?* Or: *How did the Treaty of Versailles affect the economic conditions facing a devastated Germany after World War I?* Much of our upbringing happened in our compact kitchen—tucked between two pantries in our Winsted home— and at our family table.

Mother invented a wide variety of recipes, using her own intuition and judgment, the way her forebears did. Our diet was heavy with different kinds of fresh beans, vegetables, fruits, grains, lamb, and fish. Among my favorite dishes was *Shaykh il Mihshee* ("the king of stuffed food"), a baked eggplant stuffed with minced lamb, pine nuts, and onions, garnished with tomatoes and served on long-grain rice with a tossed salad. Mother did not like fatty foods. She never fed us hot dogs, not because she knew they were bad, but because she just didn't know what was in them. She believed in serving a healthful variety of simple foods, and didn't like to fuss over food. She cooked quickly, washing her utensils as she went along, preparing food from scratch—no canned foods or processed meats and grains. And she held to the rule—*everything in moderation*—even our morning cod liver oil (yikes!).

In the Arabic language, words of endearment are derived from the world of food. "How delicious you are," parents tell their children, or "How tasty," or "How tender." Sounds funny in English, but in Arabic such comments are ancient, routine, and heartfelt. As much as she loved us, though, my mother never *asked* her young children what we wanted to eat. Why? Because "young children don't know what is good for them," she observed after we were grown. "They don't have to like what they eat; they just have to eat it." We were expected to eat everything on our plates. "If children find out that not eating will bring lots of attention, then they will frustrate their parents by making a scene again and again at the kitchen table," she said. "Parents must not lose control here, or else they will have a scene often at dinnertime." But she knew that children also have an acute sense of fair play. "Parents should eat the same food as their children," she believed. "No double standard."

I think of those words of hers whenever I'm in an airplane or a restaurant and I hear parents ask their young children what they want to eat or drink. We've all heard the worst possible responses to these questions: "I don't want soup," or "No, I hate carrots!" or, far worse, "How many times do I have to tell you, I want a Coke for breakfast! Or a cupcake! Or donuts!" Many parents seem unable to put an end to such officious rejections, and all too often surrender to their children's demands. The kiddie-food marketers have taken control of these children, and there seems to be no level of reasoning capable of breaking their hold.

Even those moms and dads mindful enough to mouth a few nutrition-is-good-for-your-body platitudes are easily defeated by a few choruses of *Why?* from their kids. The intensity of contemporary mass merchandising, aimed directly at children, has dampened their respect for the adults around them, weakening their sense of parental authority. Our family table wasn't without the occasional bout of resistance, of course; after all, kids are kids. But my mother always had a response at the ready. She knew how much we were interested in history, for instance, so if we balked at a dish that was rich in vitamin C, she would tell the story of how the sailors of olden days grew sick from scurvy until someone discovered that sucking lemons on board ship brought salvation from the disease. Or how desert Bedouins could survive for a long time on a diet made up largely of dates or figs. Most of the time, though, she would lean over us intently, looking into our eyes, and answer our *Why*s with a firm "Because it is good for you." The underlying message, of course, was: *I'm your nurturer and I want the best for you.*

And when that didn't work, Mother was capable of cutting right to the point: "What does your tongue have against your heart, lungs, liver, and kidneys?"

The family table was an ideal place to teach us manners and respect, a task for which my mother drew on her endless supply of food-related proverbs and sayings. Some of them were simple rhymes, easy to remember: *As the ship goes out to sea, I shovel my food away from me.* Others were Arabic proverbs that applied to more than table manners, like *He who takes too big a mouthful shall find it difficult to swallow* (it sounds much more melodic in the original). She preferred not to reprimand us directly, which would have been humiliating. Sometimes a lift of her eyebrows conveyed her message eloquently. But we also knew that if we ignored her signals, she would make herself clear. We learned not to take food before the guests were served, and to respect our elders by behaving ourselves at the dinner table.

Mother paid attention to the flavor of food, and to its taste, texture, aroma, and appearance—attributes that, to her, added up to its "bouquet." Her blend of tasty nutrition calmed us down and made us more receptive to the challenging conversations and stories that garnished our dinner table. Years later, when we persuaded her to write down some of her thoughts about family and child rearing—along with some nuggets of wisdom and insight from my father, and a selection of recipes from our childhood—the result was a volume called *It Happened in the Kitchen.* Phil Donahue invited Mother and me to talk about the book on his show in 1991, and we were pleasantly surprised by the response, both in the studio audience and from around the country. They loved the show's old-fashioned tempo, its plain talk, and the authentic common sense born of the experience of generations. Within days, the book had sold fifty thousand copies.

This connection was further strengthened when Aunt Angele, my mother's younger sister, immigrated to this country shortly after World War II. She brought with her the history of the twenty-five years since my mother had left Lebanon, and shared it with us at her new home near ours in Connecticut. Her hospitality and sumptuous tables were a centerpiece of our lives throughout the thirty-four years she lived there; it was there that we witnessed her love of the Arabic language, and the fondness for Arabic poetry, songs, and proverbs that she shared with her sister. At family occasions, such as weddings and birthdays, she demonstrated a distinctive talent for poetic expression herself, and further enriched our appreciation for the beauty of language.

It occurred to us that families all over our country could do the same thing we had done—to collect the stories and wisdom of their parents, grandparents, and even their great-grandparents before they are lost forever. The resource of generational history is accorded little attention in our society, which seems ever more obsessed with making "new" and "better" synonymous. From my family I became aware of the importance of passing along wisdom from one generation to the next. Yet despite the increasing proliferation of digital recording and other communication technologies, we're passing on less knowledge today than our parents did through the oral tradition alone. We're drowning in photographs and videos, capturing every mundane moment of our birthdays, holidays, and vacations. Yet these can be no more than pleasant distractions, only scratching the surface of our real relationships.

I'm reminded of all of this when I think back on our maternal grandparents in Lebanon. My siblings and I have only a few pictures of them. But the times we shared on our memorable visit there—harvesting fruit from their small orchard and garden, sharing stories around their large dinner table—gave us a lasting sense of connection to them, and to each other.

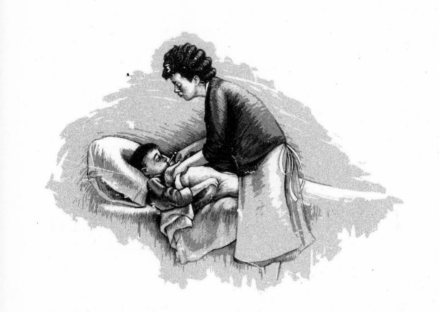

3.

The Tradition of Health

Years after we finished our formal education, we asked Mother how she'd approached the challenge of teaching us about health, which most children don't take too seriously. "There are key moments when raising you," she said, and she knew how to strike when the iron was hot. "When you were sick, I gave you your lessons on health. There was no more receptive time than when you were in the middle of chicken pox, mumps, whooping cough, and measles." As we struggled to fight off our childhood ailments, Mother's gentle admonitions about the importance of eating well and getting enough rest and exercise—and "not doing anything foolish that would damage your health"—fell on receptive ears.

Taking care of one's health from an early age was one of my mother's passions. "If you have your health, you have everything," she told us. "Without it, you have nothing." Mother had seen many health-related tragedies during her childhood in Lebanon, and she knew that the effects of neglecting one's health could appear with a vengeance years later, so she didn't believe in taking chances. Besides, we grew up in pre-antibiotic times, and our heightened awareness of the contagion of polio—then seen widely as more fearsome than cancer—made her health advice more acute and urgent. We wouldn't think of drinking out of other people's glasses, even within the family.

"Better than practicing what you preach," Mother always said, "is preaching what you practice." So she did. She ate what we ate, exercised and played ball with us, and made sure to get her daily rest, preferably in the form of an afternoon nap. But she worked hard to earn those naps: Mother used to clean her house on her hands and knees, and when she was done she would go to work in the yard and garden. We got the idea, all right. We all did our chores alongside her.

Mother had an intuitive sense of when not to rush to the doctor. Our parents always paid attention to which physicians in town were most skillful—not just the ones who were more friendly or charming, but the ones who kept learning and which ones stopped learning, which ones encouraged questions and which took queries as mistrustful of their doctoring. She had a general practitioner, Dr. Roy Sanderson, who seemed to know which parents had enough common sense to handle their children's well-being on their own and which ones needed his closer attention. You can guess in which category he placed our mother.

Though my father owned a bar as part of his restaurant, alcohol was never a staple in our household. When guests came over my parents might serve wine, and my father liked an occasional taste of *arak* with his food, but that was about it. I don't recall any beer in the refrigerator until my brother came home from the navy. Smoking, too, was a generic taboo, except for Dad, who often held a cigarette between his lips while managing the restaurant—although he didn't inhale, much to the amusement of his smoking friends. Nonetheless, he favored heavier taxes on tobacco products, and believed that doctors didn't focus enough on prevention. Society doesn't use doctors wisely, he contended, paying them merely to treat sickness, not to help people improve their health or prevent future illness. Doctors should be urging patients to eat healthier foods and conquer their addictions, he said over and over again. When he retired, he quit smoking, cold turkey.

Dad's most instructive lesson to us was his avoidance of extremes in his daily life. No matter how hungry he was, for example, or how delicious the meal my mother prepared, I can't remember a time when he said he overate. He used to tell us, especially at Thanksgiving, that the difference between a great dinner and a failed dinner was perhaps two or three mouthfuls too many. He didn't sleep too much or too little, didn't walk too much or too little, didn't try to shovel the snow too rapidly, drive too quickly, or spend too rapidly. He was the soul of moderation, and we could not help but notice.

My parents had a thousand little ways of bringing home the importance of nurturing our health. Even in this they made an example of the birds and squirrels around us, pointing out how they took care of their own. Once Pop made us laugh by reminding us that these animals were more careful with their health than the irresponsible teenagers of our area, who swaggered around as if asking one another, "Hi! Here's how I'm damaging my health. How are you damaging yours?"

Mother and Father were rewarded for their lifelong healthy habits by living into their late nineties. We never heard them make the merest complaint about aging. And when they could no longer be completely self-reliant, they received our assistance with ease and grace. For them, as well as for us, it was in the natural course of events.

4.

The Tradition of History

Our childhoods were livelier because my parents always put a premium on the lessons of history. Learning from the past, they taught us, was crucial for understanding the present and shaping the future. It was a rich journey Mom and Dad took us on—worldwide, nationally, regionally, and locally. We relished their stories of the heroes of history, though not so much for what side they were on as for the stories of what they did or said—the wise phrases of Lincoln, the gallantry of Saladin in his twelfth-century victory over the European crusaders, the liberational voices of

Arab patriots against the French and British rulers, the frugal sayings of Benjamin Franklin, and, of course, the poetry of several long-forgotten poets. Mother often shared such stories at lunchtime, when we rushed home from school—not just for the food but also for the next installment of her latest historical saga. And this storytelling approach to history whetted our appetite to read more on our own, including historical novels from the Revolutionary and Civil War to the tales of Genghis Khan.

When we children were respectively eleven, nine, seven, and three years old, my mother set sail with us for a year-long trip to visit her family in Lebanon just before World War II. While my father stayed home to tend to the restaurant, we made a voyage into history—both our own family history and the history of our ancestral home. We took in the archaeological ruins of Baalbek, and the history of the Levant under the Ottoman Empire and then under the French colonial mandate. We learned of the struggles of my great-grandparents' generation, and absorbed the cultural history of custom, myth, folklore, festivities, food, humor, and religion. We learned to see history as geography, its contours mapped in the cities and villages and terraced countryside of our ancestors, and chronicled in the ancient lore of the luscious vineyards and orchards and the very rare small rivers. Along the banks of these small rivers people still sat together, sharing food and stories. Their conversations were sometimes delicate and nuanced, sometimes uproarious, and often full of reminiscences, tapping into the past for insight into the present. Even the local small talk here drew on larger spheres of reference, including colonialism and the rebellions of earlier periods. Even chronic Lebanese gossipers talked politics.

Back in Connecticut, we paid similar attention to our local history. With the imposing Civil War Veterans Monument nearby, and a wonderful library full of history books and materials around the corner, our part of northwest Connecticut came alive with the tales of its dairy, apple, and other farms, of its many factories, and of how the great natural disasters, floods, and gigantic blizzards were overcome. It was the time of the great U.S. melting pot, a time when immigrants came here to become Americans.

As is the case today, hometown history rarely came up in our elementary and high schools. We learned it from the old-timers around us, who shared their stories in town meetings and impromptu street-corner gatherings, in sandwich shops and bars. The bustling sidewalks and the local restaurants—my father's included—were places for talk and eating; their counters and booths lent themselves to passing conversations far better than today's fast-food restaurants.

Sometimes knowledge of the town's history got me into trouble. In the third grade, when my teacher referred to the "Beardsley Public Library," I corrected my teacher in front of the class. "Miss Franklin," I said, "The Beardsley and Memorial Library isn't a public library, it's a memorial library." My parents had always stressed the importance of charity, and I knew that our library had been established in the nineteenth century through the generosity of the well-off Beardsley family and other donors. My correction got me a trip to the dunce chair in the corner. It was a valuable memory for me, but not in the way Miss Franklin intended it. It taught me the difference between instructional obedience and critical education, though I did not quite phrase it that way at the time.

The local daily newspaper, the *Winsted Evening Citizen,* was another conveyor of local history. I was a delivery boy for a time, carrying a weighty 120 copies in a sack I flung over my shoulder. Needless to say, I read what I peddled from door-to-door, and as I did I began to marvel at all the parts of this town that escaped most townspeople's awareness. Mother once wrote a short article called "Touring Your Own Home Town," in which she suggested that residents visit our numerous factories, schools, town departments, farms, our reservoir and purification plant, the rivers, streams, lakes and woods, the county courtroom and local hospital, firehouses and local landmarks, and of course, the Winchester Historical Society. Just seeing how all the various products that fueled our local economy— from clothing to clocks, from the common pin to electrical devices and household appliances—were made would be an eye-opener for most residents.

My father, who had a bottomless appetite for political news, viewed the events of history in cause-and-effect terms. To him, wars, tragedies, and elections were the result of preexisting social and historical conditions, and their consequences were all too often ignored by greedy powerful interests in favor of their immediate lust for domination and profits. This mindset led him to a political perspective that ran counter to nearly any prevailing party line. He also saw how the appeal of communism in Third World countries was nourished by callous and colonial corporate capitalism, whose political allies propped up dictatorships while the very rich oppressed the rest of the population. If the governing officials would only give a thought to the workers' desire for a decent life, he would say, "communism wouldn't have a chance." Having been born under the rule of foreign occupiers who wrote the self-serving history books the students in Lebanon had to study, he came to believe that history was written—and revised—by those whose interest it was revised to serve. Whenever he heard people say that Columbus discovered America, he would laugh and ask, "Didn't the people who greeted him on the shore arrive before he did?"

My father had an interesting take on how to accelerate the retirement of cruel dictators. As usual he started by asking me a question:

"Why don't dictators ever retire voluntarily, except to let a family member take over?"

"Because they like the power and the wealth and the adulation," I replied.

He countered by suggesting another reason: fear. Once those dictators were no longer protected by the military cordons that shielded them, they would be vulnerable to the many enemies their rule had created. Their years of brutal domination would make it difficult for them to have a second act.

But obviously there was an advantage to luring such figures out of office. So my father proposed an unorthodox solution. "Why not have the international community establish a retirement island for former dictators?" In exchange for agreeing to release the reins of power, they would get guaranteed security on an island somewhere in the South Seas or South Indian Ocean, where they and their extended families could tend their gardens or write their autobiographies. They would be forbidden to travel except for exceptional situations, and their communications with the outside world would be monitored. Since most dictators are already of an advanced age, the opportunity to escape the constant fear of reprisal might prove incentive enough to accept the invitation. Perhaps most important, scholars would be given access to them, interviewing them to learn just how they had maintained their totalitarian hold over millions of people—a subject my father found critical if mankind were to forestall the emergence of future dictatorships.

Of course, Dad's idea raised all kinds of questions: Would exile on an island paradise really be sufficient punishment for these often-murderous rulers? How could security be ensured? Who would pay to maintain the facility? But when I tried to poke holes in his "solution," he waved them away, arguing that such details could be worked out once the general plan was accepted by the proper authorities in the nondictatorial community of nations. Besides, he had to get back to work. Easy for him to say—but such conversations conditioned us to think in unusual ways.

My brother, Shafeek, shared my father's interest in history, which dovetailed with his own affection for geography. Shaf was convinced of the importance of having a sense of place—so much so that he collected U.S. Geological Survey maps of our county and its towns, which he kept rolled up on his bookshelves ready to use on his regular tours. He read deeply in American history, and like my father he enjoyed pointing out its sugarcoated versions. One day, after prevailing on our parents to buy us a brand-new set of the *Encyclopedia Americana* (the 1947 edition), Shaf pulled me aside and read a passage from the entry on Hawaii. The article referred vaguely to "external influence" that had caused tumult for "the Kingdom of Hawaii" in the late nineteenth century. "These influences finally caused a revolution in 1893, deposed the reigning queen, Liliuokalani, and established a provisional government. A republic was formed the following year with Sanford B. Dole as President. Pursuant to the request of the people of Hawaii, as expressed through the legislation of the republic, and a resolution of the United States Congress approved July 7, 1898, the islands were formally annexed to the United States on August 12, 1898 as a territory."

Shaf looked up at me when he finished reading. "Do you know what really happened? The Dole family, other Anglo planters, and some missionaries engineered a coup to overthrow the indigenous Hawaiian monarchy. This was no 'request of the people.' It was simple colonial imperialism, secured by the U.S. Marines. The encyclopedia is whitewashing history." At the age of thirteen, I found this an invaluable lesson in skepticism: Even an established encyclopedia, I had learned, could contain a political agenda. By the time I arrived in college and law school, my critical faculties had been honed by years of such exchanges with my perceptive family.

5.

The Tradition
of Scarcity

Waste was anathema in our household. Despite their comfortable middle-class income, my parents followed a policy of scarcity that went beyond even the calls for sacrifice that President Franklin Delano Roosevelt made during World War II. My parents took wartime measures like rationing and recycling in stride—and found that they provided an occasion to teach us the value of scarcity. My parents planted their Victory Garden and raised chickens during those years of food rationing, and during the war my father kept up his long-standing practice of saving string, winding it into ever-larger balls for reuse. He recycled paper and walked instead of driving, so that he could save his gasoline coupons for more necessary purposes. Mother could get more out of a bag of groceries than nature seemed to permit; she was a very imaginative kitchen manager. My parents kept the indoor temperature in our house between sixty and sixty-five degrees during the winter, to save on heating oil. Father wasn't shy about saying he didn't mind denying the oil companies a few pennies. The fact that we lived among thrift-conscious New Englanders didn't hurt.

We children learned early to shop for bargains. We watched our parents, who were both careful shoppers, and when it came time to spend our own nickels and dimes, we tried to follow suit. Of course, we did have one advantage over other children: Since Dad sold ice cream and candies at his restaurant, we never had to spend our own money on such things. When Dad opened up the spigot of his ice cream machine and let the freshly mixed chocolate or strawberry ice cream (made with fresh strawberries) spill onto our dishes, it gave off an aroma and taste I can still recall today.

Our parents taught us, in countless little ways, to control our cravings—from children's toys to household utilities. We learned to keep the lights off unless they were needed. That way, they told us, we could have brighter bulbs when the lights were on. Careful use of resources was the rule even when it wouldn't have cost us to use more. Our town's municipal water system was abundant and cheap. There was a water bill, of course, but (in those days) no meter on the amount that a home uses; we could have let the faucet run while we brushed our teeth, or used a gallon of water to wash a dish or two—but we avoided such waste as a matter of family habit.

A new toy was a special occasion, and most of them were the kind that could be used again and again—tops, crayons, picture books, puzzles, and dolls. Today's homes are often overflowing with dozens of complex, often violent electronic plastic toys, and yet children soon grow bored with them and demand the latest upgrade or fad. Bombarded with dazzling advertisements and irresistible messages, they nag their parents to buy. The result—to say nothing of what it does to our children's behavior and character—is this avalanche of *things,* of stuff that's soon discarded or left to clutter basements, attics, and garages.

That was the point of my parents' emphasis on deliberate scarcity: It taught us to value things, to preserve things, to attach our imaginations to what we had rather than to the unquenchable obsession with more, more, more. Our tradition of scarcity encouraged us to be creative. My sisters busied themselves knitting some of their own clothes, and sewed other pieces of their wardrobe with my mother. In this they were following the tradition of our aunts in Lebanon, whose skills at sewing and embroidery showed such exquisite artistry that today they might make a modest fortune as clothing and linen designers. Scarcity is far less time-consuming than abundance.

Saving time for creative pursuits is a continual dividend of not owning so many things that they eventually own you. More, we learned, was really less.

One day after he retired in the early 1970s, Dad observed that "thrift" and "thrifty" were words he used to hear all the time, but that he was hearing them less and less. Thrift and other related principles—frugality, economy, scarcity—were once a part of America's shared value system, and they were certainly part of our family's frame of mind. Today, however, millions of children are growing up with the opposite attitude, with a diminished sense of the work that goes into material things. And with such feelings grows a tolerance for wasteful economic systems, for wasteful technologies, for gas-guzzling SUVs, designer cell phones, and disposable products of all kinds.

Such designed-in waste may be profitable for manufacturers, for fuel and electric companies, and for retailers. But it hardly benefits our families, who every year hand over more of their money to the disposable economy, even as their children grow more distracted and more demanding.

As the household goes, so goes the nation.

6.

The Tradition of Sibling Equality

During our appearance on *Donahue* in 1991, Phil asked Mother how she responded when her children asked, "Which of us do you like best?" Mother replied by recalling how Bedouin mothers answered that question: "I like the one who is farthest until they are near, the youngest until they grow older, and the sick until they are well." In other words, *It depends on the situation.* Children understand that, in any given circumstance, their parents might need to show one of their siblings special treatment. What they can't accept—what can scar them for years—is when a parent shows *repeated* favoritism. This can lead to terrible consequences—withdrawal, chronic sadness, shattered self-confidence, and bitter resentment.

As the fourth of eight sisters in Lebanon, my mother learned from childhood the importance of treating every child equally. When the eighth sister was born, some neighbors and friends came to commiserate with her parents for having all girls and no boys. My grandfather was having none of it; before the Turkish coffee and sweets were served, he shooed them away with a friendly "scatter from here, scatter from here!" He would not entertain such regrets for a moment. Both of my mother's parents were champions of equal treatment for their children, and for them having eight girls was no less a blessing than having eight boys.

Children early on do sense unequal treatment by their parents. Not surprisingly, this was one of my first awarenesses as a little boy—my mother especially went to great lengths to ensure that her four children never felt they were being treated or spoken to as inferior (or superior) to one another. How did I discover this? Simple: Whether she was admonishing or praising me, she never measured me against my sisters or brother. Not once do I recall her saying, "Look how much better behaved they are," or "He's so much smarter than you." Nor did she set rules based on the idea that one of us was more or less capable or deserving than another. The only exception had to do with age: Mother did insist that the younger children should show respect toward their older siblings. As the younger brother she very much wanted me to learn from my older brother and sisters. That sibling hand-me-down learning process, she believed, would be an important source of nurturing during our upbringing. It also saved her time. Mom and Dad even welcomed my eight-year-old brother Shaf's offer to name me himself, saying that I would be his new companion.

This equality of rearing extended to the level of daily detail. That was what made it routine and therefore normal. None of us received special gifts denied others without understanding why. Similarly, at a time when more boys than girls went on to college from immigrant families, my father and mother expected us all to obtain a higher education; my two sisters each obtained a Ph.D., and the boys went on to law school after college.

As a result of this equitable treatment, we children grew up with little envy or egocentricity to come between us. The older ones helped the younger ones when we needed it—and, oh, do I remember one time when I needed it.

For my eighth-grade graduation, I was chosen to make a speech before several hundred parents and friends in the school auditorium. But as I sat in the living room a few hours before the evening festivities, I developed a terrific case of stage fright. I had planned a presentation on the life of John Muir, the great American naturalist responsible for the creation of Yosemite

National Park in California. My brother, Shaf, had recently returned from the navy, and he came over and asked what was wrong. When I explained, he sat down next to me on the sofa, and put his arm around my shoulder.

"Have you ever heard of Stravinsky?" he asked.

"Who?" I replied.

"Igor Stravinsky, the Russian composer. He wrote *The Rite of Spring*," he added. This piqued my curiosity, so I perked up, and he continued.

"*The Rite of Spring* was a very unusual composition. It opened in Paris in 1913, before a large and skeptical audience. Three or four minutes into the symphony, the crowd was grumbling; some of them started expressing their revulsion out loud. Soon there were catcalls, and that led to shouting, and then a few people even started throwing debris onstage. Others rose and stormed out of the hall. The orchestra found it impossible to continue.

"Now, Ralph, when you stand up and start describing the work of John Muir before your classmates' families and their friends and neighbors, no one is going to grumble. No one is going to speak against you. There'll be no catcalls, no shouting, no throwing tomatoes. And, certainly, no one is going to march out of the room. So what are you worrying about?" With that he rustled my hair and left the room.

Was I nervous when I finally spoke that evening? Sure. But Shaf was right: There were no catcalls, no jeering, nothing but a respectful audience and one relieved speaker when it was all over.

Was it all harmony between us? Not for a day. We argued and kidded and cajoled each other all the time. But our parents had taught us to respect each other, and we did—every day.

7.

The Tradition
of Education
and Argument

One day, when I was about ten, I came home from grade school. When my father saw me, he asked a simple question: "What did you learn today, Ralph? Did you learn how to believe or did you learn how to think?"

For some reason, that question was like a bolt from the blue. It has stayed with me ever since as a yardstick and a guide. In my adult life, I have thought back on it countless times: Is this new movement or politician trying to make us *believe,* by using abstractions and slogans or advertising gimmicks, or inviting us to *think* through the issues, using facts, experience, and judgment? It has helped me to interpret people's styles of persuasion in normal conversation—whether they are sharing how they think, or merely what they believe. And it has helped me find weak spots in countless arguments I've entertained through the years—whether in real-time debates on radio or television, or in the more thoughtful forum of the printed word.

This is not to discount the importance of belief, without which, after all, we couldn't hold to the principles and ethics that shape our daily lives. Rather, my father's point was that we should reach our beliefs by thinking them through. In public school we received instruction, which was largely a matter of belief; it was at home that we received our real education, which had more to do with thought. There was nothing wrong with this combination: Both instruction and education were the better for it.

For one thing, our parents did not draw strong boundaries between the two spheres. Over dinner, they often asked us how school had gone that day, challenging what we were learning by posing broad, open-ended questions, rather than quizzing us on matters of fact. Once, my mother and father were in the backyard with my two sisters and me. When Mother asked us how much a dozen eggs cost, or a bushel of apples, a dozen bananas, a head of lettuce, a pound of butter, and so on, we knew the answers—as children of a restaurateur and former grocer, we had a head start. For my mother, though, that was merely the foreground for her next set of questions: *What is the price for the clean air today?* she asked. *What about the sunshine? The cool breeze? The songs of the birds and the shade of the trees?* Each new question was greeted with silence, driving home her lesson—which was that what is so valuable in nature has no price, and therefore is not for sale. Later we were to learn the importance of ensuring that other elements of a just society—such as politicians, elections, and even teachers—should never be for sale either.

Such exchanges, however brief, honed our minds to be more mentally alert, to go beyond the ordinary challenges of our rote learning in school. From time to time, though, my teachers reinforced my parents' lessons. For instance, our parents were always warning us about procrastination, putting off chores that should be done on time. Then one day I walked into my fifth-grade classroom and saw my teacher, Ms. Thompson, writing something on the blackboard in her big, bold chalk letters:

LOST: 60 SECONDS
DON'T BOTHER LOOKING FOR THEM
BECAUSE THEY ARE GONE FOREVER!

Wow! That's about the most memorable episode of my entire fifth-grade education—and of my sixth-grade education, for that matter. Though I surely lost many sixty-second periods in the years that followed, never to recover them again, those words on the blackboard never left me.

My parents put a premium on our education, both at school and at home. One of the reasons my father moved us to Winsted was that the schools and library were just a few minutes' walk from home. My mother, who'd been a teacher before she married, knew full well that the likelihood of getting in trouble increased with the distance from school and home. She also liked being near our teachers. If they ever complained about our schools, their concerns focused on how much progress we were making and what our teachers thought about our performance. Were we attentive in class or distracted? Helpful or unruly? Our parents were not interested in putting us under undue pressure, or in monitoring us too closely, but they were keen to be kept informed about more than just our grades. As my father once said, "One reason so few educators pay attention to the quality of our children's education is that quality doesn't cost enough." In other words, money alone can't ensure a quality education; only deep care taken by the teachers themselves can make the difference. (Those were the days before constant multiple-choice standardized testing began restricting teachers' judgment, forcing them to "teach to the test.")

The Beardsley and Memorial Library was the perfect complement to the educational encouragement we received at home. We almost devoured that library, with its enticing variety of books, its so-appealing open stacks with their musty smell, and its helpful librarians. We could borrow three books at a time and they were treated with something close to reverence until we finished reading them and returned them for another lot. "Imagine what a bargain books are for readers," father once observed. "The author spends months or years writing a book. You reap the benefit of all that effort in just a few hours." I liked books about the Wild West and the struggles between colonizers (the pioneers, as they were called) and the Indians (whom even our esteemed Declaration of Independence referred to as "savages"). History books, books on geography, on the great inventors (Whitney, Fulton, Bell, Edison) and explorers, ancient plays from Greece and Rome and modern classics by the legendary American muckrakers (Lincoln Steffens, Ida Tarbell, Upton Sinclair, George Seldes, and Ferdinand Lunberg). These books weren't assigned by our teachers; Shaf read them all on his own (at fifteen, Tarbell's book on Standard Oil was tough going), and I followed suit. There was school time and there was library time, and not until high school, when we went to the library to research our papers and work on class projects, did the two come together.

We were not shy about bringing our newfound knowledge home, including the difficulties we had with some authors. Our father had a different take on things. If we ever came home saying we couldn't understand a certain writer or philosopher, he would respond by suggesting that perhaps the authors themselves weren't writing clearly. He was not making excuses for us; he was merely making a perfectly plausible observation that our teachers never mentioned. Excuses were a subject of passionate aversion for my mother, who was always bothered by the sight of parents trying to explain away their children's misbehavior. She always advised her friends not to make excuses for their children, for she felt that making excuses deprived children of the incentive to improve. My father used to say, "Your best teacher is your last mistake." This was a bundle of wisdom we took to heart: Like all children, we made plenty of mistakes, so therefore we had lots of teachers.

We were never able to impress our parents with the number of books we read. They were interested in what we derived from their pages, not just how many pages we turned over. They were too busy to dote on trivial benchmarks or childish academic bragging. When it came to teaching us, Mother preferred indirection to lecturing, but she wasn't above issuing a direct riposte when needed. The moment one of us began showing signs of overconfidence, she was ready with her response: "You better be a genius, because you've clearly decided to stop learning."

Many of our dinner-table arguments concerned matters of social justice at home and abroad. Often these conversations were kindled by our parents, and we were usually eager to take the bait, raising some controversial issue for discussion—such as, were unions paying as much attention to consumer prices as they did to wages? Some of these points of contention were evergreens, none more so than my father's idiosyncratic proposal for a just society based on what he called the "limitation of wealth."

For many years my father wrestled with the tension in

American society between greed and need. To address the problem, he proposed a system of unlimited income with limited wealth. Under his proposal, anyone could make and spend as much money as he or she was able, but whatever money they accumulated in savings, above a threshold of $1 million per person (in 1950 dollars), would be taxed, after a reasonable homestead exemption. To my father, this system was a reasonable way to maintain a prudent balance between economic incentives and economic justice. The very wealthy would become more interested in donating their money to community betterment (after all, how much could they consume?) or spreading the wealth among more people. Together with a progressive sales tax (with exemptions for the poorer classes) to fund governmental services, my father's wealth-limitation plan would have redirected people away from accumulating wealth toward community generosity.

Whatever their actual merits, my father's ideas had one inestimable side benefit: They kept us debating. We children spent years challenging him on its particulars, speculating out loud about how it might be made to work or why it was doomed to fail. *Isn't it too idealistic, Dad?* we would ask. Couldn't rich people avoid the taxes by taking their wealth abroad? How could such an idea ever get through Congress? What would the limitation of wealth contribute to the resurgence of communities? Would it cause people to have warmer feelings toward one another? There would be fewer spoiled-rotten descendants of wealth, we felt sure. Would this increase private investment? Savings? How much would the surge in private community giving reduce public spending? If it's so logical, why hasn't this idea caught on with some honest politicians or national citizen groups? And how do you define wealth, anyway—sure, it should go beyond cash savings to include land, buildings, stocks and bonds, but what about jewelry, rare collectibles, insurance policies? How would the progressive sales tax work?

Dad always took our responses seriously, and we would respond to his answers with new questions. But he always focused on the bigger picture—that history shows that economies with more equitable distribution of wealth were far more prosperous, with bigger markets. They were more prone to deal with the needs of tomorrow, not just today, like healthful surroundings and a better future for our children and grandchildren. "Either we spread the wealth in a country where millions of humans go without," he would say, "or we spread the misery."

In retrospect, it was like arguing with an ever-resilient law professor. He took great enjoyment from these tangos of minds. Father's limitation-of-wealth idea offered us a constant flow of discourse; like Aladdin's lamp, it needed only to be rubbed to work its educational magic. And it wasn't just at home that he would put forth these ideas, but in the workplace and anywhere he thought there was a possibility for discussion.

You may be wondering: Was there any plain old small talk in our family? Sure, there was plenty. But it was put on hold whenever we got into one of these serious discussions. At home we had the sense that there was a time and place for everything. Somehow we were never bored. When my parents had guests over, we would sit on the rug on the side of the living room and listen; every so often one of the grown-ups might make a passing reference to us, but these adult gatherings never centered on us preteen children, who were usually to be seen and not heard. By the same token, we never expected to perform or preen for the guests; instead, we listened and learned a lot about worldly matters. Looking back on these get-togethers, I marvel at how wide-ranging and informed the conversation always was: My parents and their friends traded political opinions on world and national news events, historical allusions, proverbs, and even poetry.

That was the way our "education" went: Our work at school was supported by what we learned at home, and vice versa. When I got deeply interested in stamp collecting, it was because it helped me remember the names of countries all over the world. And when I got deeply interested in my classes, it was because of a special teacher who valued spontaneous discussion over rote memorization. Many of our teachers were from Vermont, New Hampshire, and Maine, and they took their lifetime work quite seriously. There was no "gifted students" category then that allowed advanced students to take their own courses. All the students were in the same category, which in retrospect only helped our socialization as a group, while still allowing the more energetic students to excel. (On the other hand, our school buildings had no accommodations for students with disabilities, who were thus prevented from attending their area public schools. In some ways, those were years of low institutional expectations.)

Many years later, the prize-winning journalist David Halberstam, who lived in Winsted as a youngster, wrote a feature article about these teachers for the *Boston Globe;* his piece did not reflect well on contemporary urban schools by comparison. Around the same time, I was rereading John Dewey on moral education. *Eureka,* I thought: That's what my parents had given us at home. At school, we had learned facts. At home, my parents had taught us "character," which the ancient philosopher Heracleitus called "destiny." For us, they gave new meaning to the word "homework."

8.

The Tradition of Discipline

My siblings and I were raised to have respect for our mother and father—a respect born of our generations of family tradition, but also earned on a daily basis by their example. Yet of course we got into mischief, as all children do. And when we did, there were consequences.

Mother and Father followed a finely calibrated series of parental reprimands, a system that we learned early and became accustomed to heeding. It started with a sudden stern look—and often that was enough to change our young minds before things went any further. When the look alone didn't work, they relied on a sequence of three Arabic reprimands. The mildest was *skoot* or *skiti* (male or female), the next stage was *sidd neeyak* or *siddi neeyik,* and the third level was *sakru neekoon.* Translated loosely, these meant "hush your mouth" in varying degrees. If that didn't work, we might be told to leave the dinner table and/or go to stand in the corner by the sewing machine. Or we might be assigned a chore, to drive the point home in another way. Our parents rarely spanked us, and when they did, it was no more than a gentle smack on the rear. Then as now, too many children have been picked up and shaken—as toddlers, even infants—or beaten by parents losing their self-control and abandoning themselves to rage. My parents were horrified by such behavior.

But they knew the importance of enforcing their commands around the house. As my mother was known to say, "If parents don't discipline, or they're indecisive about it, their children won't respect them." It wasn't enough to issue a reprimand, in other words—not if the parent merely unravels it a few minutes later by apologizing (even tacitly) and fawning all over the child. Any child who's treated that way is being trained in the ways of manipulative behavior. "Children are clever," Mother said, "they watch their parents and can take advantage where they see weakness."

Instead, my parents chose to *show* us where we had gone wrong, and they often did so by relying on traditional proverbs. The supply of proverbs at their disposal was countless, and they wielded them effortlessly. These sayings, which came from a rich oral tradition, drew on the imagery of the past to reframe all manner of human behavior for the generations of the present and future. The villagers and peasants of their Lebanese mountain towns would have known hundreds of these proverbs; our Aunt Adma knew more than a thousand. (Think a moment: How many proverbs can you call to mind, beyond Benjamin Franklin's homilies—"A penny saved is a penny earned" or "A bird in the hand is worth two in the bush"?)

My dad, who worked seven days a week at the restaurant, used proverbs constantly. To a child talking silly, he would say (in Arabic), "Jokes are to words as salt is to food"—that is, don't overdo it. To a child who'd put off his chores too long, the apt and famous proverb was, "Wait, oh mule, until the grass grows up." When generosity was called for, he would say, "Empty hands are dirty hands." Such proverbs were admonishments, to be sure. But they also managed to teach and uplift our horizons at the same time—far more than the staccato barking of parents who shout, "Stop it! I said stop it!" or "Cut it out, now, or you'll be sorry," and then have to repeat themselves over and over while the child ignores them. Dad was a devotee of the Socratic method; he loved nothing more than to pose a provocative question and then let it hang in the air. Once, when he noticed a bunch of teenagers in his restaurant laughingly pouring pepper in the sugar bowl, he came over to them and quietly asked, "Why are you insulting your parents?" as he took away the sugar bowl. Instead of asking them to leave, he merely walked away, leaving them to ponder over his words.

Both my father and my mother were highly sensitive to the weakening of parent–child relationship in modern society—to the threat the marketplace posed to the concept of parental authority. Even back in the 1930s and 1940s, my mother noticed that some caring parents were afraid of their children, afraid of how they might react if they were disciplined. She noticed even more fear as she grew older, and often commented that "Americans are afraid of their children." She believed that children who see that their parents are afraid of them will try to control their parents, who will then begin to lose their parental moorings as a result. We were always astonished to hear a classmate slinging harsh words at his parents. To be sure, we weren't always privy to what provoked such outbursts; we just knew that in our family there were lines you never crossed. (Only later did we realize that such behavior could be symptomatic of child abuse behind closed doors—though the parents we observed never treated their children brutally, at least in public.)

When we ran afoul of our own parents, did we get a chance to argue our case? Not in trivial, run-of-the-mill situations, but when there was a meaningful disagreement at stake, yes. "When my children would explain [themselves] to me," my mother once said, "I would sometimes find that they were right, but I also explained my position." Mother believed that a child should understand why he's being told *no,* or *yes.* She always valued a good argument on a worthwhile subject. But she also believed that a child shouldn't be allowed to argue for argument's sake.

As we grew into our teenage years, our parents were more willing to engage us in back-and-forth dialogues on our little domestic controversies. But they also had subtle ways of reminding us how much they labored for our well-being, and how many years of knowledge had gone into their positions. We often, if not always, gave them the benefit of the doubt. We respected their authority, never calling them by their first names no matter what our age. But we never became overly dependent on them, either. Their unassuming confidence only enhanced our own self-confidence—until we began to seem overconfident, in which case they were quick to reply, "So, since you've got all the answers, you don't have any more questions, eh?"

There was one respect in which Mother and Father showed absolutely critical self-discipline, and that was in their interactions with each other. As children, we were aware of occasional friction between our parents. We could sense the mood changing when that occurred. But the conflict never spilled out in our presence, for our parents believed that any such display would have reduced our respect for them. They were able to keep their differences very private from us and from their friends, in part because the differences between them were mostly ordinary tensions that worked themselves out in the course of daily life. For them, the well-being of their children, which took priority over petty disagreements, served as a kind of universal solvent, dissipating any lingering tensions.

This mutual self-respect came home to us whenever we were at our friends' homes and witnessed sharp exchanges and vitriol between their parents. Sometimes, just walking the residential streets, we would hear shouting from one home or another. Once, as I was walking downtown to do an errand for my mother, I saw a door fly open, and a husband rushed out shouting curses, with his wife right behind him throwing miscellaneous pots and utensils at him along with a stream of invective. There was nothing like that kind of spectacle to help a boy appreciate his parents' efforts to preserve their emotional self-control.

As my mother often said: "If you make something bigger, it becomes bigger; if you make it smaller, it becomes smaller."

9.

The Tradition of Simple Enjoyments

Ask yourself, when do you laugh the hardest and the longest? When you're watching a situation comedy, a reality show, or a comic on late-night TV—or when you find yourself in hilarious situations with friends or family? No contest. Those bellyaching laughs come faster, and last longer, when you're with friends or family. The television shows are part of the market-driven manufacturing of laughter. Friends and family are a gift, and those personal relationships engender deeper, more truthful mirth.

We grew up in an environment of simple enjoyments, a

world largely separate from market entertainment and almost wholly diverted by family entertainment. The ways we enjoyed ourselves might appear impossibly quaint to today's youth, who've grown used to nonstop commercial entertainment so fast-paced that anything slower is greeted as BO-RING. Theirs is a video-audio, sensualized, commodified world that has displaced simple homemade pleasures, driving them down the rungs of attraction so that only the youngest children are expected to embrace them.

In our town there was one movie theater, the Strand. It had Saturday matinees for children, and we were allowed to go to the movies about twice a year. More often we headed to the Soldiers' Monument grounds, where we ate delicious sandwiches while feeling the coolness of the stone seats on our legs during a hot summer day. On Sunday afternoons we took our bikes on exhilarating rides down the tree-lined road to the nearby village of Colebrook. I can still feel the thrill of the breeze as we cruised down the long hill on our way home. Roller-skating on a neighborhood sidewalk was perfect for sunny days, but the rain didn't stop us: We just headed downstairs and skated in our basement. I even shot basketballs in that cool basement, into a bottomless apple basket hung on the staircase.

Our daily lives were full of these simple pleasures, no matter how old we were or what time of year it was. Running up to the garden to pick tomatoes or squash or beans, then back into the house to help prepare them for dinner, made us little ones feel we were part of a big act. Climbing up the venerable apple tree was a blast, and plucking the insect-scarred apples left us with small but very juicy bites. (Nobody had to tell us the apples were "organic"!) Just the thought of eating Mother's home-made pastries, whose aroma wafted from the oven to the kitchen table, made our mouths water.

Winter brought the crunch of a white Christmas, even as we walked to midnight service at the Episcopal Church. Mother would take us outdoors and teach us the alphabet by carving letters in the snow. As we grew older, we sledded to school on snowy mornings. Then, come Easter time, my mother would hard-boil dozens of eggs with onion skins, staining them dark red. After they were all hidden, we would go running around finding them—and then compete to see which egg would survive what we called the "cracking competition." Each of us would make a wish, and then crack our egg up against one of our siblings' eggs. We looked forward to the cracking competition for weeks.

Summers were an exciting time; we all looked forward to a change of pace. When we were little children, Dad would take us up to Highland Lake, where we'd go driving over the spillways between the lake and the spill of water down the valley into the Mad River, cruising through half a foot of moving water. "Wheee!" we'd cry. "Turn around and do it again, Dad!" Then he would take us up to Crystal Lake, the bucolic town reservoir, where we would look out over the water with a kind of reverence. Coming from the Middle East, where water is scarce and deserts plentiful, our parents taught us to view abundant clean water with gratitude.

We spent our summer vacations with our Aunt Adele, my mother's older sister, and her six children. She and her husband, Selim, lived in Toronto, Canada, and we alternated summers with her family, spending one summer in Connecticut, the next in Canada. Our age-matched cousins were like another set of brothers and sisters, and our aunt and uncle stepped in as surrogate parents. Our families were not only extended but amplified by the sheer variety of personality and experience our cousins brought to the mix. Their lives were different from ours in a hundred small ways: They wore school uniforms and we did not, followed hockey where we followed baseball, pronounced English words differently—and such differences made for endless hours of fun and argument.

Though our parents had ten children crammed into our relatively medium-sized house during those summers, I never remember hearing the mothers complaining about the extra work, or even saying they felt especially tired. The older children helped them with the cooking and cleaning chores. And having two sets of parents certainly helped preserve order: When it came to being disciplined or taking instructions, we listened to and obeyed our aunt and uncle as surely as we did our own parents.

Our house had a screened-in porch upstairs, with room for three or four beds in summer, another memorable setting in our childhood landscape. Even the children of the next generation, beginning with my sister Laura's children, always relished the chance to sleep on the exalted porch. It was seen as a first-class treat. At night we could hear the crickets, see the stars and the moon and the clouds, tell stories, engage in horseplay, laugh, while my mother and her sister were visiting downstairs, entertaining each other with their own stories of childhood, and news from home. They would tease each other, and the gales of laughter would come wafting through the windows. Now and then, when it sounded as though we were getting too boisterous up on the porch, one of the sisters downstairs would say, "That's enough, children. Go to sleep." That would usually quiet us down—but not always. Then they had to come up to the porch to enforce this point

Our mother and aunt each felt free to compliment or admonish any of us as they saw fit, and this had the effect of reinforcing many of our family's traditions. Whenever we came to them to settle a conflict that cropped up among us, they were both equally likely to offer up one of the sayings they learned together in childhood: "It doesn't hurt to be generous," or "Don't judge until you know the whole story," or "If someone does you harm, do him some good"—advice we'd all find useful throughout life, and all passed along in a way that was memorable, short, and sweet.

When it was our turn to travel to Canada, we usually joined Aunt Adele's family in a cottage on Lake Simcoe or Lake Couchiching. The routine would be less varied than when we were together in town. But those weeks we spent together were more attuned to nature. They were shaped by our closeness to the water, by afternoons spent swimming on a beachfront just down from the cottage, by boating, fishing, hiking, picking berries, games of hide and seek in the woods. My mother and her sister knew how to delegate responsibility to the older children, trusting our older cousins to keep an eye on us when we went to amusement parks in Toronto.

As we grew up and went to college, these joint summer vacations became less frequent. But we all remember them fondly, and in the 1980s Shaf organized several summers with our cousins and their families at Georgian Bay, so that a new generation of children could get to know each other in the setting that had meant so much to us when we were youngsters.

Amid all this, though, I must confess that there was one commercial enjoyment I never tired of—one that lasted well into my teen years. That was taking an early morning train from Winsted down the Naugatuck Valley into Grand Central Station, and then transferring onto the subway to Yankee Stadium to watch my favorite team clobber the opposition, especially the Boston Red Sox. You see, our town was divided right down the middle, half being Yankee fans and the other half being patient Red Sox fans. My boyhood hero Lou Gehrig, the "Iron Man," had recently retired from the Bronx Bombers, but he was still fresh in everyone's memory, particularly after his tragic illness. Returning from a ball game at Yankee Stadium meant hours of banter, joshing, and tireless arguments with the misguided Red Sox fans in the neighborhood.

Of course, all these and innumerable other simple pleasures are available to many youngsters today. But the screens and earphones are taking over—the video games and iPods and television and all kinds of salacious websites. The only electric distraction we had was the radio, and that was offered to us as a reward, not surrendered to our control as a daily routine. Instead we contented ourselves playing kick-the-can in the backyard, or hitting fungo balls to each other on the sandlot baseball field, playing marbles, or hiking along streams in the woods. It was certainly cheaper than the ceaseless parade of gadgets parents are obliged to purchase today, and you could play the same game again and again without being bored or demanding an upgrade.

There was something about playing with the same building blocks that invited encore after encore. What was that something? My guess is that it was the fact that we were interacting with other human beings, not with machines. We were tapping into the infinite richness of human senses and emotions, challenging our imagination and human competitiveness, rather than the staccato rhythms and predictable rewards of pre-programmed games. This blend of the familiar and the surprising gave us all the joyful feeling that we were making our own pleasure—not relying on structured "playdates," but having our own fun.

10.

The Tradition of Reciprocity

Out of the confluence of these previous traditions grew a subtler, deeper tradition, a second-generation tradition that ensouled our family to the present day. It was more than mutual respect. It was more than mutual aid. I think of it as the tradition of reciprocity.

Underlying the help and comfort we extended to each other, as needed, was the fact that we all cared deeply for one another. I felt this caring in a variety of unexpected ways. One day, when I was five years old, my father took me by the hand and walked me down to the Fourth School, the local elementary school. My father knew that I'd already moved beyond the kindergarten level, and he convinced the school that I should skip kindergarten and enroll as the youngest pupil in Miss Root's first-grade class. I overheard the case he made, and when I realized how much he believed in me, I became utterly determined not to let my father down in front of other people. Within days I was Miss Root's assistant, helping some of the students with their lessons. (Decades later, when she was in her eighties, Miss Root recounted this story to a television magazine show.) In class after class, through high school, I would look back at the class following ours and be so grateful that my parents had cared enough to move me forward. Whenever the work grew challenging, that awareness would inspire me to work even harder.

My parents always saw their relationships with their children as mutually rewarding. They raised children who could teach their parents in turn, sharing their own experiences and insights. As young adult immigrants (both came over at the age of nineteen), my mother and father knew that learning shouldn't end with childhood; they spent years absorbing a culture, a host of new technologies, and systems of private businesses and public institutions—all in a foreign language. This has never been an easy process for newcomers to our land—even after finding work, they often don't have it easy. So-called generation gaps are especially common among immigrant families; these gaps can produce anxious and unpleasant tensions, and sometimes lead to nasty ruptures or chronic conflicts.

Many children of immigrants feel embarrassed at their parents' "old ways," their accents, their native language being spoken in their friends' presence. They have little patience with parents who don't keep up with teenage fads, rejecting the elements of their traditional lifestyle in favor of the easy social bonding of commercial culture. The parents, in turn, sometimes feel rejected, isolated, and worried. Some grow so disconsolate that they return to their home countries.

My parents, on the other hand, were quite practical. They sensed that their children were becoming a part of this new world, and set about following their example. Who better to teach them about America, they reasoned, than their children, who had never known anything else? My older brother, Shaf, was my parents' most conscious interpreter. He always had a bent for anthropology and cross-cultural awareness, even during his teen years, and when it came to American culture the child became the teacher and the parents became the students (until it was time to say "yes" or "no" or "be careful," that is). Sometimes the teaching went both ways, with surprising results for both sides: When my sister Claire tried showing my mother how to dance the Charleston, Mother responded by singing a song about the Charleston in Arabic and English that was popular in Lebanon in the 1920s.

From time to time Shaf ran into resistance, as when he tried to persuade my mother that some new movie at the Strand would be all right for his younger siblings to see. Like many parents today, Mother was wary of Hollywood and its sexy movies

embarrassing her early teenage children. (She never for a moment worried that they could actually *corrupt* us, only that we'd
be made uncomfortable.) To her, sexy and violent movies were
demeaning and wasteful, and she wanted to spare us from enduring them if she could. Obviously, there were times when we
disagreed, thought her too protective of us, but we never did
anything that showed disrespect toward her final say on the subject. Some time ago I was pleased to learn that this feeling had
moved to the next generation, when her grandson Tarek told
me that he'd decided in college never to do anything he would
later regret.

My father even extended such reciprocal relations to his
customers. The one day Dad's restaurant was supposed to be
closed was Christmas Day. But my siblings and I soon noticed
that every Christmas morning he would go down there at
eleven o'clock and spend three hours serving a few longtime
customers—elderly renters who lived by themselves and relied
on him for their daily lunch.

That was the example both our parents set for us, and in
their final years their kindnesses were returned in their moments of need. My mother had always been one of the most
self-reliant and independent people I'd ever known, but by the
time she was nearing her one hundredth birthday, she finally
needed help to get around. My sister Claire was there to care for
her, and she treated the responsibility as if it were a privilege to
extend her hands to embrace our mother's needs. Claire rejected
the bureaucratic term "caregiver." To her it was a much simpler

matter: "She is my mother," she would say, "and I am her daughter and we respond to each others' needs."

As the weeks passed, and mother needed more assistance, not once did Rose Nader ever suggest that she was a burden on her children. She had cared for us all during our infancy, childhood, and adulthood. Of course, we would be there for her at the very end of her life. She viewed her life as a state of oneness with her children and grandchildren. And oneness cannot be a burden on itself.

11.

The Tradition of Independent Thinking

"Turn your back on the pack," I remember my mother telling me more than once during early childhood. Simple words, but they carried a few meanings in a very concise way. If we wanted to be leaders, we were taught—if we wanted to think boldly, and to excel at what we did—that we would have to be willing to be different. My mother took a continual interest in who my friends and acquaintances were from year to year. She encouraged us to bring our friends home, and when we did, she would engage them in conversation about school, their families, or the aspects of their lives that mattered to them. Even in those relatively quiet, unfrenzied, drug-free small-town days, she was keenly aware that peer groups were her competition in rearing her children. A child's peer group could be very influential, and the wrong group could dash years' worth of attentive child rearing and proper behavior. Peer pressure could be nerve-wracking for children, especially when it involved coercion, as it often did when there were age differences in "the pack." My mother's saying *I believe it's you!* always comes back to me in this context: She taught us early that we couldn't pass off on others responsibility for our own behavior. "Respect yourself," she taught us, "and others will respect you."

Well, as children will, we understood our parents' words, but still listened to our classmates' taunts, and we weren't immune to them. I was eight years old before I finally confronted my mother about the fact that she still had me wearing short pants to school every day. She believed I was too young to wear long pants, unlike the other boys who wore them. The boys in my class thought short pants were babyish, and I agreed. So one day I brought my odd-boy-out lament home to my mother. After trying out all kinds of practical arguments to shuck the shorts and wear the longs—such as protecting my knees from scraping falls or being warmer in the cold winters—I realized I was getting nowhere. So I brought out what I perceived as my trump card. "Mother," I entreated, *"their mothers* let them wear long pants!" To which mother replied: "Well, they have their mothers and you have yours. Besides, why are you worried about being a little different?"

Word gets around quickly in a small town. Before meeting these youngsters, Mother would inquire about their parents and their older siblings. She had a short list of children who were absolutely off-limits; but generally she let her opinions be known, and we followed her lead. Other mothers did the same for their children—and sometimes to our detriment. One mother disapproved of her blond son walking to school with me because of my "darker complexion." Winsted, like many New England factory towns, was by then a multiethnic community; the nineteenth-century influx of Irish and Italian immigrants was followed by Eastern European, Greek, and Levantine families. In the town's restaurants and bars, ethnic jokes were common currency; such mutual ribbing probably helped to reduce some tensions, inasmuch as they teased each other face to face. But there were some prejudices manifested in terms of social distance and less occupational mobility for the newer families. The Yankees still held the economic power in Winsted, but Irish Americans and Italian Americans were beginning to play a part in local politics, where there was a strong perceived division between Protestant and Catholic families.

The smaller ethnic groups felt the most discomfort. Our family could have been in that category. I say "could have been" because our parents were predisposed to ignore such pressures, joking about them while shoring up our identity and self-confidence by condemning prejudice itself. Having the largest restaurant in our small town didn't hurt, either: Food can be a great leveler, and the easy interactions in a bustling eatery—which served American food, by the way, not ethnic fare—made for a forum where politics and sports were all debated on an even playing field.

My father had come to realize this years earlier, during his time in the melting pots of places like Newark, New Jersey; Detroit, Michigan; Lawrence, Massachusetts; and Danbury, Connecticut. "What is the true value of ethnic identity?" I remember him observing once. "Culture, humor, variety and a common sociability for facing life. And, of course, the pleasure of having one's own cuisine. When it comes to politics, though, a broader humanity should replace ethnicity."

So how did this play out on the children? Ethnic slurs bounced off us because we knew who we were, where we came from, and generally where we wanted to go. From time to time, we heard someone use a phrase like "camel-driver"—as some anti-Arab voices still do in America today. But such language only singed us when it was associated with rejectionist behavior or tied to social distance. Fortunately, such moments were infrequent. Our teachers were quite even-handed, and we played sports and did odd jobs around the neighborhood with no complaint. The simple fact that we spoke and understood Arabic did, of course, make us different. But our parents' accented English only gave us something in common with the numerous

Italian, Polish, European, Jewish, and the few immigrant Lebanese families in town.

Given all this, our parents were remarkably easy in the saddle. They never became overwrought about perceived peergroup pressure or bigotry, and even seemed to understand the old-time families' sensitivities toward the unfamiliar newer immigrants and their customs. The public schools and especially the churches helped newer families like ours assimilate into the community; our family had been embraced by the Methodist Church, even though we came from the Eastern Orthodox division of Christianity. Ultimately, as my father understood, our ethnic differences tended to shore up our defenses against prejudice and temptations. We knew the value of our history, and relished the elements that came with it—the food and humor especially.

12.

The Tradition
of Charity

Every major religion, and many minor ones, level charitable injunctions on their followers. For centuries, the concepts of tithing and good works have been central to Christianity. Beyond charitable giving, the scriptures are filled with homilies, exemplary narratives, and other stories enshrine the duty to act generously and compassionately toward one's fellow human beings. Though we did attend Sunday School at the local Methodist church, our real education in the meaning of charity came from the largely secular tradition of our parents and grandparents—one that dated back at least as far as my maternal grandmother, a leading doer of good works in Zahle, whose prompting had led to the construction of a hospital in the town.

This tradition crossed the ocean and took two distinct pathways. One can be called "point of need" charity, in the form of things like the free food and hot coffee my father gave readily to the poor when they came to the restaurant. Especially during the Great Depression, hungry people would go door-to-door begging for food. When they knocked on our door, Mother happily directed them to our restaurant, with the assurance that a hot meal would await them. The expression of gratitude on their faces made a deep impression on our conscience.

Father considered it his responsibility as a businessman to extend such help to those in need, which is why we children always treasured the following exchange he had in the late 1940s with a local doctor, a friend he bantered with often at the lunch counter:

DOCTOR: Why are the auto workers' wages so high?

FATHER: So they can afford to pay your bills! Why do you charge so much?

DOCTOR: Because we often treat poor people free.

FATHER: (Smiling) Well, in that case, since we give free coffee to poor people, your coffee [then 10 cents] today is $1.00. Thank you.

Dad did not think of his charitable activities as something to be pawned off onto the backs of his other customers.

Another example of his charitable impulse occurred during World War II. His office tenant above the restaurant, Dr. Henry Garbus, a dentist, was called to military service. Dad held his office free of charge, pending his return, and refused to rent it to someone else—even in what was then a high-demand market. He told Dr. Garbus that when he came back to his family after the war, he would find his dental office just as he left it. All he would have to ask for were the keys before restarting his practice. Nearly three years later, that is what Dr. Garbus did. When it came to the war effort, Dad believed he had to do his part again and again on the home front for those who were in the armed forces.

The second path had to do with systemic charity—in the form of building or expanding facilities and institutions that benefited the community. For example, in the mid-1950s, although the restaurant business was not doing all that well, my parents gave what was for them a major donation to a charitable fund being raised to build a large new wing to the local hospital. Mother took a special interest in the project, joining other Winsted donors to go and watch the new construction. She also talked up the fund-raising drive in the community, going door to door, as she did often for the Red Cross. Later I heard her comment in passing that "we built the hospital," and there was quiet pride in her voice. "You should care" was a mantra in our household, a conviction that found expression in myriad ways.

Once, when an elderly neighbor fell on the ice and broke her arm, Mother sent my sister Laura, who was about eleven years old, to help her dress. She cried and didn't want to go but she went anyway. Sometimes you have to do things in life whether you want to or not.

Even with their obligations at home, my parents still found a way to extend their charitable giving back to their homeland. When my father's home village in Lebanon needed a new sewer system built, he sent his own money for the project, and collected donations from other Lebanese immigrants in the area. He followed up that project by helping to persuade Winsted town officials to build a modern sewage treatment system that would help the town kick the habit of dumping the sewage in the Mad River, which ran through the center of town!

One bright summer afternoon, Dad took me for a ride around town. I suspected there was a purpose to this trip beyond catching the breezes by the lake or watching the teenagers playing sandlot baseball near the high school, and I was right.

First, we drove past the Beardsley and Memorial Library. Ellen Rockwell Beardsley had started this institution in 1901, he told me, with a donation of ten thousand dollars—a princely sum at that time. He then drove up Spencer Street until we got to the Litchfield County Hospital—the first such institution in the county in 1902, when it was built, and also a product of private charity. Down a few more roads to the other end of town, and we were at the Gilbert School, a high school that for years was regarded as among the best in the nation. The Gilbert

School was launched by a local industrialist, William Gilbert, who built the world-renowned Gilbert Clock Company in Winsted. His original gift established Gilbert as a private secondary school, the Gilbert School, but it gradually became more public over the years as more tax dollars were used to supplement a declining endowment.

Turning left, my father drove up a hill to Highland Lake. Nearby there was a small inviting park with some seats and tables for having outdoor lunches—a park established by another local philanthropist. Then we made a 180-degree turn and drove down toward the long Main Street—passing the Winchester Historical Society, founded and nurtured with charitable contributions. He drove past some other charities, including the imposing Gilbert Home for orphans and other needy children, and arrived at the beautiful Soldiers' Monument, so central to my childhood imagination. The town had paid a dear price in casualties during the Civil War, and after the war ended a volunteer veteran and local philanthropist promoted the idea of such a memorial; it was finally dedicated in 1890. With several donated acres of hilltop land, the structure and its grounds soon became a haven for the townspeople, who still conduct summer theater there, and whose children frolic on its grounds or run around the perimeter.

When we'd finished our tour of the area, my father pulled up to our house and turned the ignition off. "See all those fine establishments in our little town?" he said to me. "Think about how important they are to our community. Then ask yourself this question: Since 1900, there were and are at least a hundred townspeople as wealthy as those philanthropists were. What kind of town would this be if those people put some of their wealth back into the community the same way?" We sat there together in silence, a light wind breezing through the open windows. While I've since traveled many miles to many places, I've never forgotten the lesson I learned on that one trip.

On another, much later trip, I remember hearing a speaker quote Jean Monnet, a post–World War II advocate for the European Union. "Without people, nothing is possible," Monnet had said. "Without institutions, nothing is lasting."

Today, even though community-building philanthropy is tax-deductible, there are relatively fewer large-scale donations to create new institutions such as libraries, performance halls, museums, health care centers, and recreational facilities. Reliance on the government as the first source of funding for these kinds of projects, it seems to me, weakens the expectation that wealthy people will extend the legacies of their enlightened forebears, which so enriched people's lives. Our communities are diminished as a result.

13.

The Tradition of Work

We learned about work at an early age. Every one of the children was expected to pitch in and contribute daily to the smooth functioning of the household. The boys mostly worked around the house, shoveling snow, cutting the grass, raking the leaves, taking care of the chickens in and about their coop, and collecting the eggs. The girls worked mostly inside, cleaning rooms, ironing clothing, washing the dishes, and performing weekly chores such as polishing the dining room set. Girls and boys alike helped their parents with the vegetable garden, weeding, watering, and harvesting. When we became teenagers, our responsibilities grew: Shaf began working part time in Dad's restaurant after school, and I had a paper route for a while. Claire and Laura augmented their household work with serious piano lessons ($1.50 a lesson) from a wonderful piano teacher, Miss Ann Breshnan, who lived two blocks away on Main Street.

The task of ensuring quality control fell to our mother, who monitored our efforts for what she called "the finishing touch." Mother's efforts sometimes produced mirth, sometimes grumbling, as she sent us back to do the job all over again, or at least finish what we'd started—as with cutting the grass and raking it thoroughly together for compost. She viewed these tasks as strong fibers within the daily fabric of our family, something we came to understand when a heavy rainstorm or a blizzard came along to pose us a challenge. There's nothing like nature to bring about a swing-to-the-emergency camaraderie, even among easily distracted youngsters.

We were never given an allowance, for our chores or for any other reason. Our parents saw allowances as inducing divisiveness, inviting nagging (for increases), and likely to produce reckless spending. It was far better, they believed, to preserve the household as a place of shared responsibility, instead of making it a place of monetary transactions and having them pay for our work. And they believed that giving routine allowances would dull us to the meaning of money. Instead, we were obliged to ask our parents to buy things that caught our eye, forcing us to make a good argument as to why they should say yes—something an allowance would have circumvented.

They did, also, want us to learn how to save. So when we

earned some money outside the home, or were given money by relatives for birthdays or Christmas, they arranged for a savings account—at first in a symbolic piggy bank, later in the local savings bank—where we could deposit the proceeds. The little bank book in our name was a source of pride, for us and the other local children who were encouraged to save. The head of the Winsted Savings Bank even walked the kindergarten class to the bank to deposit their dimes and quarters.

Now, I'm not saying we always did our chores cheerily, or punctually. I know I sometimes grumbled when the call came to get going on cutting the grass or some other task. I would have preferred to keep reading or keep listening to the Yankees and their marvelous announcer, Mel Allen, on New York's WINS. So after the first call I would temporize. The second and third calls became more audible and insistent. Only when I heard my mother's footsteps heading into the living room did I suddenly decide I could skip the next inning or put a marker in my book. It always amazed me how fast the grass grew, the leaves fell, the chickens had bowel movements. But down deep I knew we all had to pull our weight for the greater good of the family, and that thought got me past these faltering moments. We children didn't know it at the time, but this was our education in the work ethic: Our parents were giving us far more than they themselves had back in the old country, but they were just as determined not to spoil us in the process. We had to earn it, to taste some of the exertion required for that better life.

Of course, not all the work was unpleasant. An afternoon

spent baking in the kitchen was hardly a chore. My sisters were more attracted to learning the baking arts from my prolific mother than I was, and as a result they not only learned to make celestial Arabic pastries and bread, but also absorbed all the lore surrounding the celebratory baking events that preceded religious days and festivals in old Lebanon. They also got first dibs on every new item that emerged fresh from the oven. (I did manage to bake twenty-one bran muffins for my sister Claire's twenty-first birthday, which my parents delivered to her at Smith College, where she was a student.) And of course Shaf knew how to do everything, in and out of the kitchen.

For me, it was watching my Dad work his long hours in the restaurant—solving every kind of problem you can imagine, from a failing boiler to a no-show cook to a sudden surge of impatient customers—that showed me what hard work was like, and the patience and ingenuity it takes to run a small business.

I was astonished at how many things there are to worry about when you're running a restaurant/bar. Supplies coming on time, the food kept fresh, equipment kept in good running order, all kinds of services kept up—my father carried these and other concerns on his back. He was on his feet so much every day and night that, over the years, his tired legs bulged with varicose veins, the painfully visible evidence of his intense commitment to support his family and save for his children's college and graduate school education. But the workplace was also a joy because he could engage his customers from far and wide in talk about community and public affairs.

When it came time for me to start working, I knew I wasn't cut out for the restaurant business. Thankfully, my mother and father agreed. It was while I was working my paper route for the *Winsted Evening Citizen* that I got my first feeling for the obligations of daily work—and a taste of the excitement of small-town journalism. The papers were still warm as I piled them into my large satchel. Then it was off on my door-to-door delivery rounds, warding off dogs, braving inclement weather, chatting with family members eagerly coming to the door for their paper, collecting the weekly billings and getting glimpses of how people were making it through the day, sometimes pleasant and sometimes unpleasant. How could anyone not develop an ease with people under such circumstances! When it came to meeting regular people, it was the next best thing to being a postman.

Nothing speaks to my parents' view of work better than a story my sister Claire recalled. One day, when she was quite young, she was walking home with Dad when they passed a street cleaner. "I'm glad I'll never have to do such dirty work," she cried out. Dad stopped and looked at his little girl. "Then you should always respect street cleaners," he said, "if only because they're doing work that you don't want to do, but that you very much want to have done. This is the same reason they should be paid well. Claire, as you grow up, you'll see all kinds of work being done. Don't look down on people for the work they do—and don't be in awe of anyone, either." Laura had similar conversations with Dad.

Though it would be years before my sisters shared these stories with me, I'd long since absorbed those lessons. Without the labor of millions of low-paid, unrecognized workers, I realized, the economy—along with the activities of the wealthy—would come to a halt.

14.

The Tradition
of Business

On August 19, 1955, after several days of steady rains, the cumulative effect of Hurricane Diane struck Winsted, pouring water into the Mad River. True to its name, the river swelled up quickly, overflowing its banks and destroying the businesses along Main Street. The nearby Still River joined in, rushing over its banks and severely damaging the North Main Street part of town.

Most of the damage occurred in a terrifying twenty-minute surge of raging waters. Cars were tossed around like ten pins. Several people lost their lives. Along the mile-long west side of

Main Street, the stores, apartment buildings, and factories were either washed away or crumbled from the force of the rushing waters. On the east side, which included my parents' restaurant, there was serious damage: the first floors of the buildings collapsed, and the carefully designed window displays and interior spaces were swamped by six feet of mud.

The next day the sun came out. The merchants up and down the street viewed the devastation in stunned silence. Years of their labors and millions of dollars of their investment had gone down a river that turned into a Moloch.

At the time I was in California, having finished a summer job in Yosemite National Park right after graduation from Princeton University. I was about to head home when I walked into a store in Bakersfield, California, looked at the front page of the newspaper—and saw a large picture of my father's ravaged Highland Arms Restaurant, done in by Hurricane Diane. I made it home in time to help dig the mass of mud out of the premises.

Shaf and Laura, who were there at the time of this Great Flood, told me later how my father had reacted to the devastation. Coming down the hill that morning, after just barely escaping the flood water the evening before, he surveyed the flood damage. He turned to Laura and quietly said, "It is a good thing I put my money in the children's education." Then, speaking with a few other forlorn retailers he'd known for years, he said, "Well, we'd better get to work. There is much cleanup and rebuilding to do. We can use the opportunity to beautify Main Street."

Think of it: At age sixty-two, having already endured one giant flood in his lifetime—the storm of 1938, which destroyed his restaurant—my father hardly wasted a moment looking back. He just looked ahead, to a future that was unknown or at least uncertain. He did his part to get the storekeepers in a heads-up frame of mind.

There was no flood insurance in 1955. Only the Small Business Administration came in to help with low-interest loans. By then, my siblings and I were all in our twenties. But the way our father reacted in those desolate days after the flood taught us much about reacting to adversity. He was cool, practical, and immediately focused on recovery.

Growing up in a small-business family was a significant factor in our daily lives. The Highland Arms was far more than a simple restaurant. It offered three dining areas, counter service, a cocktail lounge/bar, a delicatessen, and a bakery. Over the years, tens of thousands of customers dropped by to assuage their hunger and slake their thirst—many of them from around the country and around the world, but the majority from within the community. Suppliers came by regularly to deliver the raw materials for the kitchen and bakery. Plumbers, electricians, and carpenters came to keep the place in repair. Jurors from the county courthouse down the street were brought there on their lunch break. Factory whistles at noon brought workers there for a sandwich and coffee. Lawyers, doctors, policemen, accountants, insurance agents, bankers, teachers and school principals, summer camp managers and their campers, children and parents, poor tenants on Main Street, storekeepers—they all coursed through the Highland Arms.

The Highland Arms could fit two hundred patrons comfortably, which is quite large for a town of ten thousand. The premises became a community gathering place, in part because it was spacious enough that no one felt rushed to give up their tables for new customers. Moreover, Nathra Nader was the embodiment of vigorous free speech, and in the atmosphere he created there, free speech was contagious, combined with a wry sense of humor. *Want to express your opinions without getting a cold stare in return? Go to Nader's.* And they did, from 1925 to 1969, when Dad retired and closed the business.

When you grow up in a family business that is open seven days a week, you can bet it becomes a tradition in your life— especially when the business is so inherently personal, so constantly conversational, so insistently pressurized with daily deadlines. We grew up with long-time employees who became part of our education, wittingly or unwittingly. Our customers loved them, and for us they were a kind of extended family. There was Benny Barton, the chef who was forever talking about returning to his home in Damariscotta, Maine. It took him more than twenty-five years to do so, and in the meantime he gave his customers quality food with great reliability. There was Paul Randazzo, funny and a little flamboyant, who cooked away in the kitchen except when he suddenly disappeared for one of his unexplained absences. And so many others: Homer, the superb dining room waiter, collecting dime tips faster than a slot machine could spit them out while he shared stories about his French Canadian days; Jake Stankiewicz, the nighttime baker, who was so steady, kind, and proud of his daily creations.

Though I never longed to take over the restaurant, I did try my hand at the many skills involved, from dishwashing to short-order cooking to waiting tables. I soon grew comfortable behind the counter, talking, arguing, and joshing back and forth with all kinds of people from all kinds of backgrounds in every kind of mood. I developed an ability to read people, catching their expressions, learning about their troubles, and sharing in their spirits. I wish I knew how each of these countless interactions contributed to shaping my personality, but I'm certain that, in one way or another, most of them did. I do know that the experience helped me enormously in my career as an advocate, teaching me to communicate with sources in our investigations, as well as with the political and media people we had to deal with regularly. Those random exchanges with friends, neighbors, and strangers in the restaurant made the work of my adult life far easier to handle. I couldn't help feeling bad for my friends and classmates, who were missing out on this vital part of their education—on this immersion course in the thoughts and feelings of working people from all over the mosaic of America.

Watching my father in business also gave me an education

in the meaning of character. He had the most wonderful relationships with his longtime builder-carpenter, Bob Morgan; his longtime plumber, Ed Hutton; and others he called on for help in maintaining his restaurant and repairing it after the floods, fires, and other periodic damage. These were relationships built on trust, and an easygoing mutual respect. (Mr. Hutton even enrolled McNader into his Scottish clan!) Nothing was ever set down in writing. Their word was their bond.

The floods and fires often left Dad with business debts that took years to pay off, and his meticulous drive to do so—assisted by his Ben Franklin-worthy frugality—became a minor legend in town. Even so, his frugality never conflicted with his charitable giving. Rather, it only gave him more leeway for charity. Less waste, more giving.

As the owner of a nearby shoe store once said, at Nader's a nickel bought you a cup of coffee and ten minutes of political talk. Lots of social issues were tossed around, catching the attention of the customers and helping the local residents get both informed and stirred up. That was one contribution Dad's business made to our small town—along with many others, including a community college that was inspired by Shaf's wide-ranging conversations at the Highland Arms. To my father, the business and the community were one and the same.

15.

The Tradition
of Patriotism

Father was an incessant critic of power—business and governmental, local and national—and one who was never afraid to propose a solution. He spoke his mind daily at the restaurant. "Nathra, how do you expect to make a profit if you keep speaking out that way?" his longtime customers and friends sometimes cautioned him.

"When I sailed past the Statue of Liberty, I took it seriously," he replied.

My parents prized the freedoms they found in America, and were always alert to anyone who might try to degrade them.

My father used to say, "If you do not use your rights, you will lose your rights." And use their rights they did—by speaking up at lively town meetings, by visiting town hall officials and newspaper editors to promote their opinions, by exhorting people to be informed and to vote. Their subjects of concern were mostly local, covering the gamut of typical municipal issues: services that were needed or wasteful, schools and hospitals that needed upgrading, roads and parking facilities that needed improvement, flood-control measures that needed updating, factory dumping that needed to be policed—everything you might expect, from unleashed dogs to unreasonable budgets.

As Americans by choice, my parents never let the haughtier descendants of earlier immigrants make them feel defensive. They treasured the ideals of democracy, but they never felt compelled to accept its imperfections in practice, or to genuflect before anthems or flags. They saw right through politicians who tried to cover their sins with the Star-Spangled Banner. They cared only about how their elected officials fulfilled their duties, whether they actually engaged with the citizens or just shook hands with them in passing. As Dad often reminded the flag-wavers, our flag stands for the principles embodied in the last words of the Pledge of Allegiance—"with liberty and justice for all."

Instead, our parents found allies in the town's more active older citizens, whose experience they eagerly absorbed. These neighbors helped acquaint them with the steps of small-town governance, explaining how long each step in the process was

likely to take. Their common sense of injustice quickly over-
came any prevailing ethnic or class differences. These were the
people who knew that democracy and its benefits take work.

Father relished having a voice and being heard, especially
when he believed that his opinions could be the basis for legal
changes. For example, he once filed suit in federal court to
change the Connecticut primary system so that all voters could
participate in any primary—not just party members, who were
members of what he considered private organizations. So long
as these party primaries were being paid for by our tax dollars,
he reasoned, all voters should be able to vote in any primary.
The judge who heard his case found no constitutional right
being violated and decided against him, though other states
have such crossover primary laws.

On another occasion, knowing that consumers could buy
into group life and auto insurance, my father fought an anti-
competitive state law, lobbied by the insurance industry, that
prohibited group homeowners insurance. He wrote the Connecticut Insurance Department asking them to urge the legisla-
ture to repeal the law, which had been pushed by the insurance
companies, and pave the way for neighbors to pool their resources and save on premiums by purchasing as a group. The
Insurance Department rejected his request.

Did losing faze him? No, it merely made him more stead-
fast against any restrictions of rights or corruptions of government. It is as if he was saying, "You are not going to take away
what I came to this country to breathe."

On occasion, his nonconformist viewpoints led even his regular lunch-counter customers to question his patriotism. "Love it or leave it," they would say—but such taunts were his cup of delicious tea. He loved turning the tables on his challengers.

"Do you love your country?" he would ask with a quizzical smile.

"You're damn right I do."

"Well, why don't you spend time improving it?" he would respond.

Mother put us children through a similar drill "Ralph, do you love your country?" she asked me when I was about eight.

"Yes, mother," I said, wondering where she was going with this.

"Well, I hope when you grow up, you'll work hard to make it more lovable."

This, in our eyes, was the real definition of patriotism—as expressed by the people themselves, not by their manipulative rulers and plutocrats. When you come from an authoritarian country or worse, you tend to be much more sensitive to symbols of *la patria* being used to repress people and their participation in power. You measure your new country according to its own self-professed high standards.

A nation, our parents believed, should be judged in much the same way as an individual: by deeds, not words. Politicians and the government show their regard for our society, our community, and our fellow human beings by what they do—by their efforts to stop trouble before it starts, and to restore order or repair damage when it's over. Mother and Dad were aware that songs, symbols, and pledges, however sincerely meant, were often used as shortcuts, as substitutes for the hard work of democracy, the sweat it takes to pursue justice. And they would not be intimidated from pointing this evasion out again and again, in part because they knew that inaction plays into the hands of the barons of power and money. They intuited what Marcus Cicero said over two thousand years ago in ancient Rome: "Freedom is participation in power."

16.

The Tradition
of Solitude

For a time, my father worked from ten o'clock in the morning to two in the afternoon. Then, after an afternoon nap, he would return to the restaurant at five o'clock in the evening, and work until one in the morning. During those naps, we children had to find ways to amuse ourselves without making much noise. And yet we never had any trouble finding things to do. We were used to being left alone, to read or play quietly with our toys, to build projects or knit things, to climb trees, to walk in the nearby woods, or just to daydream. Compared with today's overscheduled children, we were used to a certain amount of solitude. And we enjoyed it.

The diversions we had in our hours alone were simple and rewarding. There were always new books to read, of course. There were chores to do, tasks that became more time-consuming as we grew older. And there was the radio—one radio—on which we listened occasionally to Jack Benny, *The Lone Ranger, The Shadow, Fibber McGee and Molly,* Lowell Thomas and Edward R. Murrow for the news, and on Sunday evening *One Man's Family.* We also had time to play outside, and time to think and muse. The philosopher James Harvey Robinson pointed out that the minds of children can reap lots of future benefits when they are permitted time for reverie. As I noted earlier, Shaf urged me to read Robinson's book when I was only thirteen, and the author's words about reverie made me feel good; until then I'd been convinced I was merely wasting time.

One reason that my parents put such emphasis on solitude was they valued their own solitude, their own time spent by themselves or with other adults. Their love for us was immense, their caring demonstrable, but they thought it was wise not to become totally absorbed by their children. As a result, we never threatened to dominate the proceedings when my parents entertained at home. We were accustomed to spending time by ourselves, and we felt little need to show off, for their sake or for ours. After a dinner with guests, we excused ourselves and went off to play with the guests' children or on our own.

Needless to say, things have changed. Some years ago, we invited a family with two small children over for Thanksgiving dinner. The four-year-old boy spent the whole day running wild, jumping off the table, knocking over glasses of water, screeching at the top of his lungs, and generally making every effort possible to ruin the conversation and the meal. Today, most parents might ask: Was he suffering from attention deficit disorder? No, the *parents* were suffering—from an unwillingness to control their son's unprovoked behavior and lay down some markers. It's a symptom of today's sprawled economy that many children spend less time with adults, including their parents, than any previous generation in history. When they do have a few precious moments with adults, they often act out as if they're desperately trying to make up for the prolonged inattention.

"I believe that children should have some time to themselves," my mother once said. "This is what I intended when I told my daughter Claire she could not sing in the choir, with a group, until she first learned how to sing alone. I wanted the children to be able to exercise their minds and understand the importance of solitude, to be self-reliant, to think independently. The children were encouraged to be themselves, to know how to define themselves." Ralph Waldo Emerson would have approved.

Of course, our ideas of solitude today can be deeply flawed. Many parents plant their children in front of TV, video games, the Internet, or other electronic child-seducers for hours and hours every week. Solitude originally meant "a state of being alone," not a state of passive symbiosis with these frenetic and often lurid temptations. True solitude can involve an infinite variety of experience: being alone with one's imagination, one's thoughts, dreams, one's puzzles and books, one's knitting or hobbies, from carving wood blocks, to building little radios or model airplanes or collecting colorful stamps from all over the world. Being alone can mean following the flight of a butterfly or a hummingbird or an industrious pollinating bee. It can mean gazing at the nighttime sky, full of those familiar constellations, and trying to identify them all.

Being alone was easier in those days. The telephone didn't ring incessantly; compared with today, it hardly rang at all. We certainly weren't besieged by salespeople calling to interrupt at dinner time. Silence was common, a phenomenon that might have flummoxed many of today's fidgeting, electronically conditioned children. Children today suffer from shortened attention spans and reduced person-to-person interactions, and the results are wreaking havoc with their ability to think, converse, conduct themselves in family life, and educate themselves. Some of these youngsters are beginning to recognize such deficits in their lives. Maybe they are looking for what Alice Walker has called "quiet space."

Contemplating what "quiet space" did for me is an educated guess, another source of wonder. Yet I know that even in childhood I treasured and relished my solitude, not as an escape or expression of alienation, but as a time for exploration and self-reflection, a time to get to know myself better. Solitude was my engine of renewal, the steward for my self-reliance and the clarifier of my thoughts. And, perhaps most important, time alone allowed me to commune with my favorite authors—the American muckrakers of the late nineteenth and early twentieth centuries, who demonstrated the importance of challenging powerful interests, and the authors of adventure fiction, who inspired me to explore uncharted terrain and expand my vocabulary of words and ideas. Although I can't say I thought in these terms as a child, it's clear to me now that my mind was always led back to things that involved making a better life for the community. I was fascinated by people who broke new ground, and wanted to do the same.

17.

The Tradition of Civics

My parents' philosophy was rooted in what might be described as the "civic golden rule"—that neighbors should treat neighbors as they themselves would like to be treated. A deep personal sense of civic duty isn't usually the result of enduring didactic lectures, much less of studying bloodless civics books. True civic awareness is a flowing river with many sources—some as small as rivulets and brooks, some as large as tributaries. In our case, the flow began at a young age, as we accompanied Mother and Father to the local town meetings where the community made its decisions.

At these meetings, our parents—and anyone else who lived in the town and cared to participate—had the chance to talk with the town's elected "selectmen," as the local representatives were called. A holdover from early New England history, the town meeting was a more pristine form of local democracy that has had no equal to this day. The public business of the town was put on display, and those townspeople who showed up regularly had few inhibitions about airing their opinions. When there was disagreement, nothing was sacred. An interested party would hardly think twice before calling out his opponent in purely personal terms: "Your father, Greg, would turn over in his grave if he could see what you're doing here."

Even as a boy, I noticed that these gatherings were often dominated by the same few voters, who took to the floor meeting after meeting and always seemed unusually well prepared for the occasion. By the time I was a teenager, helping out in the restaurant, I realized that these leading citizen activists were widely viewed as mavericks, and that some considered them oddballs or even deviants. The day after a tumultuous town meeting, people would point out Mr. Franz, a particularly motivated older resident, walking down Main Street. It was as if he were one of a trio—the town drunk, the town fool, and the town citizen. Who is more foolish, I wondered—the core group of committed voters and taxpayers who engage in the process, or the much larger number who habitually abstain from town affairs, leaving their interests to be decided by others? Later I was delighted, and not a little vindicated, when I discovered that the ancient Greek word "idiot" referred to civic apathy, not intelligence.

On the other side of the ethical tradition was the Golden Rule, and a host of similar pronouncements in the Bible that enhanced that simple call to help and get along with one another. For Dad, that was enough as a frame of reference. In the daily soapbox that was his restaurant, he was happy to discuss anything under the sun with his patrons, whether local or out-of-town. From local tradespeople to campaigning politicians, few survived a visit to the Highland Arms without having a vibrant conversation with my father. Those politicians were his special target; his counter, with its long row of seats, was an irresistibly efficient way to shake hands with a captive audience of voters. Dad always lay in wait down by the end of the counter, near the large coffee urns. And when his and the politician's hands clasped, he wouldn't let go until he had his say and got some response.

There's little doubt that, in the nearly fifty years he ran the restaurant, my father educated, motivated, and inspired tens of thousands of people to think more deeply about the issues that affected them as citizens—right there in Winsted, and around the country and the world. To this day, I still meet people from near and far who recall their conversations with him. He covered much ground in these encounters—from colonialism and the suppression of self-determination to government waste, from the shortcomings of the press to the improper relationships between government agencies and big business that favored them over small businesses, from the constant problem of inadequate parking on Main Street to the unnecessary demolition of buildings such as the classic railroad terminal at Winsted. He was constantly struck by the human capacity for greed. Dad was frequently dismayed by the performance of our presidents, the cowardly behavior of the major political parties, the willingness of Congress to vote itself large pay raises, and the exclusion of independent voters like himself from parts of the electoral process. He had a special reserve of contempt for chain stores and their migrant managers, who always came with excuses from central headquarters in New York or Chicago concerning why they couldn't contribute to local charities. The list goes on and on.

Father's zest for public debate was equaled only by his appetite for problem solving. He was a demanding citizen. In his daily round of civic conversations, he did more than just toss around the questions of the day. He helped orient and mobilize many local residents into taking action, whether through voting or protesting excesses such as Congress's large, ill-timed pay raises for itself. In 1978, at the age of eighty-six, his protest march attracted national media attention. When critical town services were being proposed, such as building a new hospital wing or a modern sewage system, he got into the debate on the ground floor, and stayed involved through completion.

He also made people think about aspects of civic engagement to which they might otherwise have given little consideration. He was fond of reexamining the conventional meaning of words—pressing his customers to think of "wealth," for example, in terms of not just money or possessions, but also charity, health, happiness, and justice in a community. He felt sorry for the very rich (even as he trounced them), pointing out that they lived in what he called a "gold cage." He never prejudged any customer to be beyond his interest, or beyond the reach of his arguments. The firmer they appeared to be in their views, the better he liked it. He was not into convincing the convinced.

My mother's civic life covered a very broad range of involvements, from the usual charities like the Red Cross to the larger subjects that are faced by every community—issues involving health, children, public works, and the like. From the time she moved to Winsted, she was struck by how insular people could be, especially when it came to international affairs. So she joined the local Women's Club, and helped to start an international committee that brought well-known speakers to address the club and its guests. When my older brother was stationed in Guantanamo Bay, Cuba, during World War II, Mother attended Spanish classes. And she became the first volunteer teacher of Arabic in the state's adult education program, which earned her a statewide television interview before any of her children had achieved any public attention.

As my mother well knew, the ethical fiber of a community is nourished by every small instance in which its citizens stand up for what is right. She encouraged her neighbors to write letters to the editor of the local newspaper, the *Winsted Evening Citizen,* but never hesitated to bypass that process and call the editor herself if she thought it would get quicker action. Mother really knew how to work the phones, in conversations that were

short and to the point. Once, when the librarians at the Beardsley and Memorial Library were having trouble getting young
people to return books, the local McDonald's offered to give a
free hamburger to children who returned their borrowed books.
Mother thought this was wrongheaded: Children should be
taught to return books to the library on time because it was
their responsibility, not because of some commercial (and
caloric) incentive. She complained, and she prevailed.

When the monstrous Hurricane Diane demolished much
of Winsted's Main Street in August 1955, she sprang into action. The storm forced the local theater to shut down for re-
pairs, and when Mother realized that the young people of the
community would need another recreational outlet, she
promptly organized social programs for young people at the
YMCA. But she also had her eye on a larger necessity—prevent-
ing this kind of disaster from happening again. Given the Mad
River's history of overflowing its banks, Mother realized that
only a dry dam could protect the town from reliving the devastation with each future storm. So she pressed for a dam to be
built a little north of Winsted, to tame the river.

For help, Mother decided to call on an acquaintance who
had a connection to Prescott Bush, the state's Republican senator. Would the senator press for a dry dam? Alas, came the re-
port, Bush responded with no more than a smile.

But my mother wasn't discouraged. One day, their mutual
friend invited Senator Bush, the father and grandfather of presidents, to speak in the area. Mr. and Mrs. Nader went to hear

him. After his speech, my mother went over and introduced herself. As she was shaking hands with him, she said, "Senator Bush, Winsted needs your support in getting the Army Corps of Engineers to build a dry dam to prevent future flooding."

Bush smiled, but said nothing.

Mother always loved recalling what happened next. "I wouldn't let go of his hand," she said, "until he promised to help." She had a tremendous grip.

And that, as it happened, made the difference. With the senator's help—and no doubt that of others—the Army Corps of Engineers did build that dry dam. There hasn't been a flood since.

"If you want to get a politician to stop smiling and start promising," she always said, "just don't let go of his hand." In other words, be persistent.

As children growing up in such a civically conscious atmosphere, we could have rebelled against our parents, as some children do. Instead, we were inspired to follow in their footsteps. Why? Perhaps because they led more by example than by didactic direction. They never took us by the shoulder and *told* us to be active citizens. We were simply immersed in the process from childhood, and we saw the results. What's more, we saw how much my parents *enjoyed* their involvement, no matter how controversial it got. The process had its ups and downs, of course, but their even tempers and sense of perspective always carried them through in good spirits.

From my parents, I learned the essential qualities that define the civic personality—a blend of constant curiosity, inventive thinking, resilience in the face of obstacles, and a willingness to share credit with one's deserving colleagues. Of course, there are also countless skills that can, and should, be learned—everything from how to interpret and disseminate a legislator's voting record, to how to use the Freedom of Information laws, to how to put on a good news conference. But in my years of public life I've found that it's those other, intangible qualities of human personality that usually make the difference—and that are so often the legacy of one's family upbringing. No well-padded war chest, Ivy League education, or cutting-edge technology can take the place of such a personality, of such commitment.

Of course, there's no deliberate family recipe, or lesson plan, that can produce these traits. Some children will always want to rebel, and perhaps for the good; many more will simply go on with their daily lives, trusting that others will carry the weight of activism and engagement. But I feel sure that raising civically responsible children is most likely to happen in the kind of atmosphere my parents created: one of indirection and delights, strong examples and certain boundaries, solitude and conversation, witness and respect, and, above all, the strength of parental love and sacrifice. All of this cannot help but nourish a sense of dedication to help one's fellow human beings achieve a better life. And once this dedication takes root, it is likely to evolve into a self-starting maturity, into a personality that seeks out struggles for fairness and gets involved.

As I look back on our society's history, on our high points of civic courage and justice, it's clear to me that many of our greatest civic leaders must have been raised to engage with the world around them in just this way. Such values are what drive ordinary people to achieve extraordinary results. And, despite my concerns about the future, I am convinced that these "natural" leaders are still all around us, in each new generation, inspired by their sense of justice and eager to bring about change. These are our public citizens—the architects, movers, and sentinels of a functioning, successful democratic society.

When I meet these confident, steady, refreshing figures, I like to ask them how they became the people they are—how they developed such drive, such motivation and purpose. Quite often, they hesitate, then smile, and respond:

> *Well, when I was young, my parents . . .*
> *my mother . . .*
> *my father . . .*
> *my teacher . . .*
> *my neighbor . . .*
> *told me . . .*
> *took me . . .*
> *showed me . . .*
> *inspired me. . . .*

For democracy cannot flourish without putting an arm around the shoulders of the young.

AFTERWORD

If you have read this far, you may be wondering, what kind of children did all these traditions produce? I may not be the right one to ask; such questions require subjective answers, and mine would be biased in a way I find unbecoming. What I can do is describe the paths taken by my two sisters and brother.

My brother Shaf, who passed away in 1986, was a student of anthropology and then of law. He was a practitioner of community economic development, the spark plug for an industrial park, and a lifelong proponent of local democracy. He did not believe that the way to effect real change was to start at the national level; much of what happens there, he believed, only served to concentrate power in ways that infrequently benefited the people. Change, he believed, must start at the local level. For this reason he was a champion of community colleges, which took their relations with the community seriously. He was the principal founder of the Northwestern Connecticut Community College, in Winsted, Connecticut, which celebrated its fortieth anniversary in 2005, and he went on to work in the community college movement nationally.

Claire received her Ph.D. in public law and government from Columbia University. Her thesis was a front-running work on the relationship between science and government, and she followed this with early research on energy conservation with a group at a national laboratory. She coedited and coauthored an early book on science and technology and development in Third World countries, and also wrote scholarly articles concerning health and safety regulation for science and technology. She started a number of citizen groups and projects dedicated to fostering systemic change and democracy at the community level, and works with them to this day. For many years Claire chaired the Council for Responsible Genetics, founded by MIT and Harvard scientists who wanted to develop ethical and legal frameworks for the momentous technology of genetic engineering. After the closing of our local hospital, she was instrumental in mobilizing the citizenry to restore health care services in Winsted, Connecticut, under a creative arrangement based on community control. Thus the Winsted Health Center Foundation was born.

Laura received her Ph.D. in anthropology from Harvard University and went on to become a professor of anthropology at the University of California at Berkeley. Her annual course on "controlling processes" has been a magnet for thousands of students. Through her fieldwork, writing, and teaching, she has been a leading scholar in the field of law and anthropology and of the hierarchies of power and control in industrialized cul-

tures. She has served on commissions to develop more enlightened policies for all our children, and on several energy policy
commissions that led the way in advocating sane energy policies. Her eldest daughter is a lawyer who defended children in
court and then turned her interest to family, home schooling,
and community. Her son has a doctorate in ecology and does
hands-on fieldwork toward the biological and cultural preserva-
tion of tropical forests. Her youngest daughter, also raising a
family, has a Ph.D. in infectious diseases, and is currently a
working laboratory scientist in the area of cell destruction and
cancer.

Laura's children maintain a keen sense of civic interest and
responsibility, something they share easily with their friends,
fellow citizens, and their own children. Like their older family
members, they believe in talking about matters that matter,
about events that affect or afflict the human condition. They
use words like "just" and "unjust." They ground their arguments in fact, and display an abiding passion for liberty with responsibility and for freedom with fairness. They believe that
deeds legitimize words, and that there can be no authentic pursuit of happiness without the pursuit of justice.

I shared their youthful enthusiasm. When I was a high
school student, I remember reading a quotation that was like a
path of light for me. It was Senator Daniel Webster's description
of justice as "the great work of man on Earth." Webster understood that no society could be improved without effort. Em-

barking on the journey I found it hard work, to be sure, but sublime gratification as well. There is great joy in pursuing justice—and that joy should be available to everyone.

Children develop their notions of fairness at a very early age. In their innocence, they are often able to imagine a world without poverty, war, or pollution far more easily than their elders. They have no axe to grind, which gives them a wonderful clarity and optimism. Through their words, deeds, and traditions, my family gave me the gift of believing in such ideals. Their strengths were my metabolism. They propelled me to try to reach as many people as I could, and to try to show them that most of our problems had solutions, if only people would give themselves enough time to stand up and be counted, and if only some of us would stand tall and lead.

For the people do have that power—but only if they recognize it, and then take the time to apply it. That is the biggest "if" in politics, isn't it? But that is the best reason for trying to make the flowers of democracy bloom.

There is an ancient Chinese proverb whose words I carry with me everywhere I go, one that captures the spirit of my parents' legacy: "To know and not to do is not to know."

Mother and Father viewed our activities during adulthood with a modest equanimity. When I emerged onto the national public scene, and started making regular appearances in the national media, their reaction could be summed up this way: "Okay, Ralph, if there's anything harder than becoming famous, it's learning how to endure it and keep on track without letting it swell your head." David Halberstam's mother and mine were friends, and he tells a story along similar lines: The first time I appeared on the cover of a major national magazine, Mrs. Halberstam called my mother early Monday morning to congratulate her.

"Really?" my mother replied. "I think I'll go out and get a copy."

David could only chuckle. "What modesty," he mused. "If I was on the cover of *Time* magazine, our family would have emptied out every newsstand in Litchfield County."

Perhaps it was my father who best captured their attitude. Once, when I told him that I'd done my best at something, he leaned over quietly and looked at me. "Son, never say you did your best, because then you'll never try to do better."

Our parents always intended to place us on productive, stimulating pathways, to guide us along until we began to pick up the pace ourselves, and then let us go when they felt their work was complete. Mother used to tell other young mothers in the community that if a child's parents haven't done a proper job by the time their child reaches six or seven years of age, their challenges will only be compounded. "The earlier, the easier," she would say—and not just when it comes to learning languages, she added with a smile.

There are millions of healthy two-parent and single-parent families who are still guided by traditions as rich as my parents' were. Of course, there are also millions of families who struggle daily under social, economic, or cultural pressures that are urgent enough to crowd out all other concerns. Today, more and more families are farming out their responsibilities—feeding their children and entertaining them, educating and counseling them, providing day care and advice—to commercial service providers. The "family industry" is swiftly becoming a real factor in our economy. And this comes with a price, as more parents lose confidence in their own judgments, in their ability to make decisions without the help of the "experts." As corporations deliberately encroach on the parenting of our children, and children spend less personal time with their parents, those all-important traditions are falling by the wayside.

Still, just as young people continue to attend Shakespeare's plays and to perform them, for many the verities and the frailties of family life are still instinctive, as they have been since time immemorial. In these pages, I hope more parents will find reasons to start rebuilding their connections with their children—by reaching back through the generations, drawing on their family heritage, and passing along the lessons they themselves learned as children. What better way to provide the climate for nurturing what Thomas Jefferson called "an aristocracy of virtue and talent"? If today's parents are to fulfill their acknowledged desire to leave each generation stronger and healthier than its predecessor, cultivating these transcendent family traditions is a good place to begin.

ACKNOWLEDGMENTS

For a volume of recollections and reflections about our family traditions, acknowledgments rest deeply on my parents, sisters, and brother, to whom this book is dedicated. More immediately, my gratitude extends to my sister Claire Nader for her on-point contributions, and my sister Laura Nader's anthropological insights. My nephew Tarek Milleron made precise suggestions in his review of the manuscript.

Special thanks to my colleague John Richard and to my editor, Calvert Morgan, whose skill as an editor is rendered finite only by his limitations of time.

BOOKS BY RALPH NADER

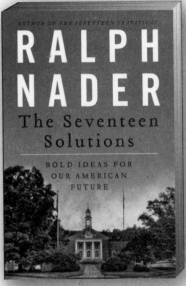

THE SEVENTEEN SOLUTIONS
Bold Ideas for Our American Future
ISBN 978-0-06-208353-1 (paperback)

From one of the most important and provocative progressive voices in American history comes a new and uplifting program to rescue America from its social doldrums. In *The Seventeen Solutions*, Ralph Nader surveys the stark, concrete contrasts between the kind of society and economy America can and should have, and the unjust conditions under which so many people actually live today.

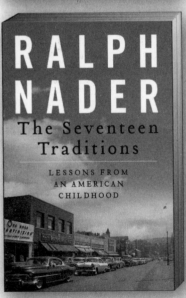

THE SEVENTEEN TRADITIONS
Lessons from an American Childhood
ISBN 978-0-06-221064-7 (paperback)

Activist and humanitarian Ralph Nader looks back on his small-town American childhood and the traditions that shaped his worldview. Weaving memoir with thoughtful inspiration, Nader reawakens our own memories of a simpler time and celebrates the enduring values that informed his perspective on politics and gave him the courage to spend decades crusading for change.

"*The Seventeen Traditions* brings us back to what's important in life—and what makes America truly great."
—Jim Hightower, *Illinois Times*